SOFTBALL RULES IN PICTURES

G. Jacobs McCrory
Revised and Illustrated by Michael Brown

A Perigee Book

Perigee Books
are published by
The Putnam Publishing Group
200 Madison Avenue
New York, NY 10016

Copyright © 1987 by Mary Ellen Morrison
All rights reserved. This book, or parts thereof,
may not be reproduced in any form without permission.
Published simultaneously in Canada by
General Publishing Co. Limited, Toronto

Previous editions (by A. G. Jacobs) 1959, 1974, 1976, 1978.

The Official Softball Playing Rules reprinted by permission of the Amateur Softball Association of America.

Library of Congress Cataloging-in-Publication Data

McCrory, G. Jacobs.
    Softball rules in pictures.

    1. Softball—Rules. I. Brown,
Michael J., date. II. Title.
GV881.2.M23   1987   796.357'8   86–25427
ISBN 0-399-51356-6

Printed in the United States of America
     5 6 7 8 9 10

CONTENTS

Foreword	5
The Game	7
The Pitcher	13
The Batter	19
When the Batter Is Out	23
Base Running	30
When the Base Runner Is Out	44
Appeal Plays	53
Umpires	58
Official Softball Playing Rules	61

FOREWORD

This book is intended for the softball player, manager and umpire. Its pictorial format and simple language offer an entertaining and enjoyable way to learn the sometimes technical and complicated official rules of softball.

A thorough knowledge of the rules is very important for the player and manager. For the umpire, it's an absolute necessity. We hope that *Softball Rules in Pictures* will help novices learn the game's rules and also serve as a handy preseason refresher course for veterans of the game.

A complete set of slow pitch and fast pitch rules can be found in the *Official Guide* published by the Amateur Softball Association of America, 2801 NE 50th St., Oklahoma City, OK, 73111.

THE GAME

THE FIELD

Softball is played on a diamond-shaped field with bases located at each corner of the diamond. The field is divided into the infield, within the diamond, and the outfield, beyond the diamond.

The field is also divided into fair territory, the area inside the foul lines, and foul territory, the area outside the lines. The lines themselves are in fair territory. **(Rule 1)**

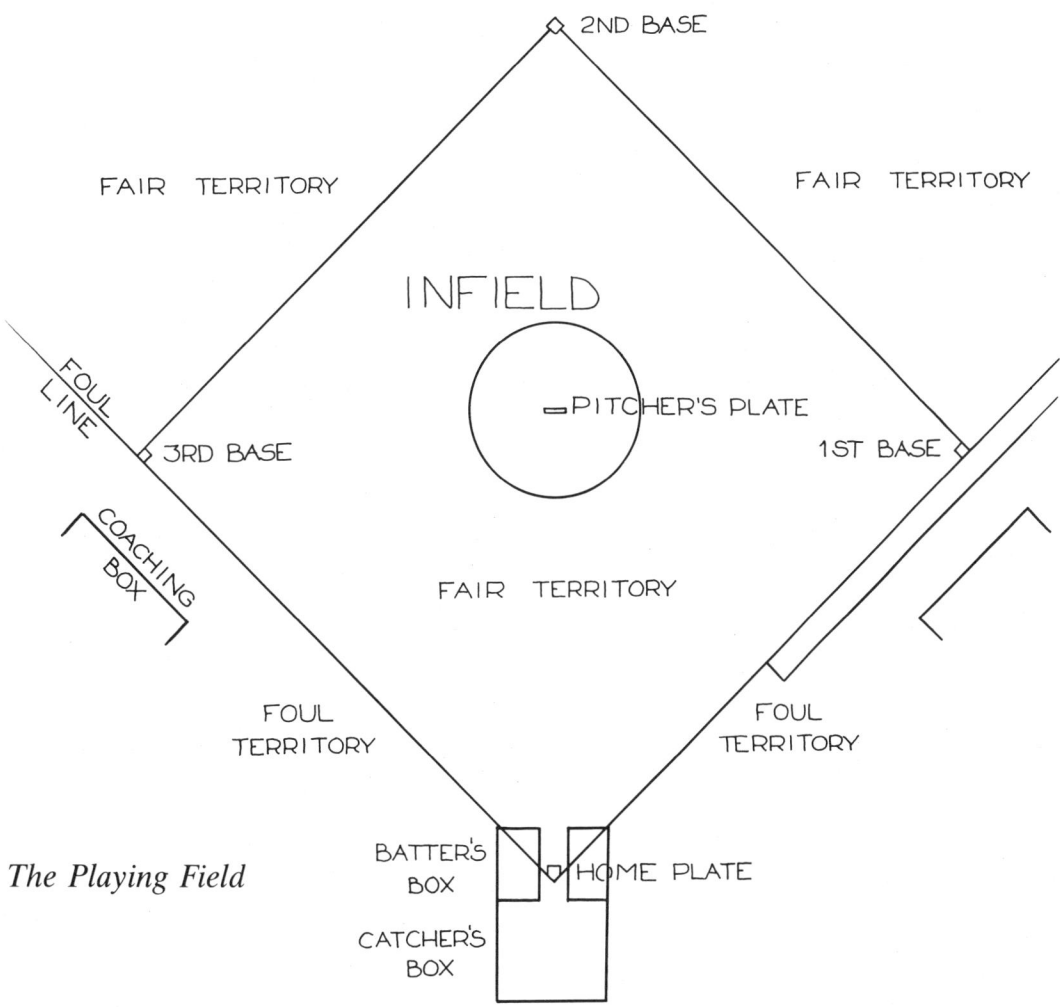

The Playing Field

There are two slightly different kinds of softball: fast pitch and slow pitch. Fast pitch is played with nine players on each team, slow pitch with ten. The tenth player serves as an extra infielder.

In fast pitch softball, the outfield fence should be 225 feet from home plate; in slow pitch, the distance to the fence should be 275 feet for men and 250 feet for women.

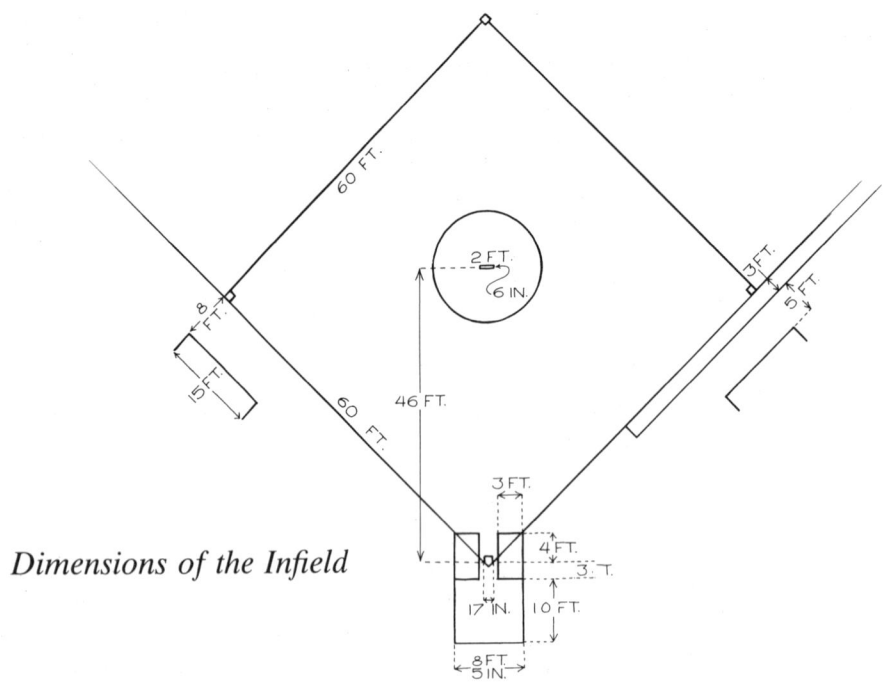

Dimensions of the Infield

THE GAME

The object of the game is to score runs. Each run counts as one point.

Runs are scored each time a batter becomes a base runner and, running in a counterclockwise direction, safely touches first, second, third and home bases. The base runner must touch home plate before the third out of the inning is made against his or her team in order to score. **(Rule 5, Section 5)**

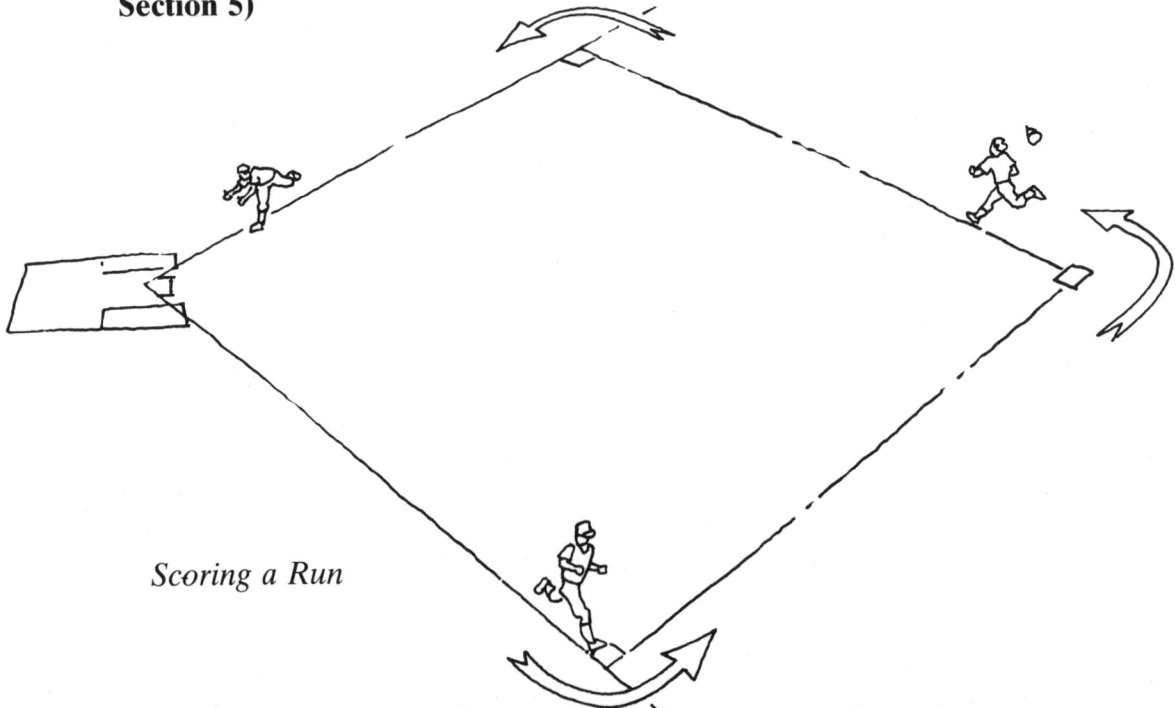

Scoring a Run

The pitcher and catcher must be in position before the pitcher is considered ready to pitch. **(Rule 6, Section 1c)**

The offensive team is the team at bat trying to score runs; the defensive team plays the field trying to stop them. Most of the players on the defensive team may be stationed anywhere in fair territory. Only the pitcher and catcher must start the play from their assigned positions on the field.

The game is divided into innings. In each inning, each team has one turn at bat (offense) and one in the field (defense).

Each team is allowed three outs while at bat in an inning. After three outs, the team that was in the field comes to bat, and the team that was batting takes the field.

The batter has just hit a fair ball. **(Rule 7, Section 8)**

A batter becomes a base runner when he hits a fair ball or is awarded a base or bases.

There are seven innings in a regulation softball game, however, there is no need to play the second half of the last inning if the team that bats last in the inning is already winning.

If the game is tied after seven innings, additional innings are played until one team has more runs than the other at the end of a complete inning.

For record keeping purposes, the score of a forfeited game is 7-0.

EQUIPMENT

Regulations govern the size, weight and shape of bats, balls, gloves and bases.

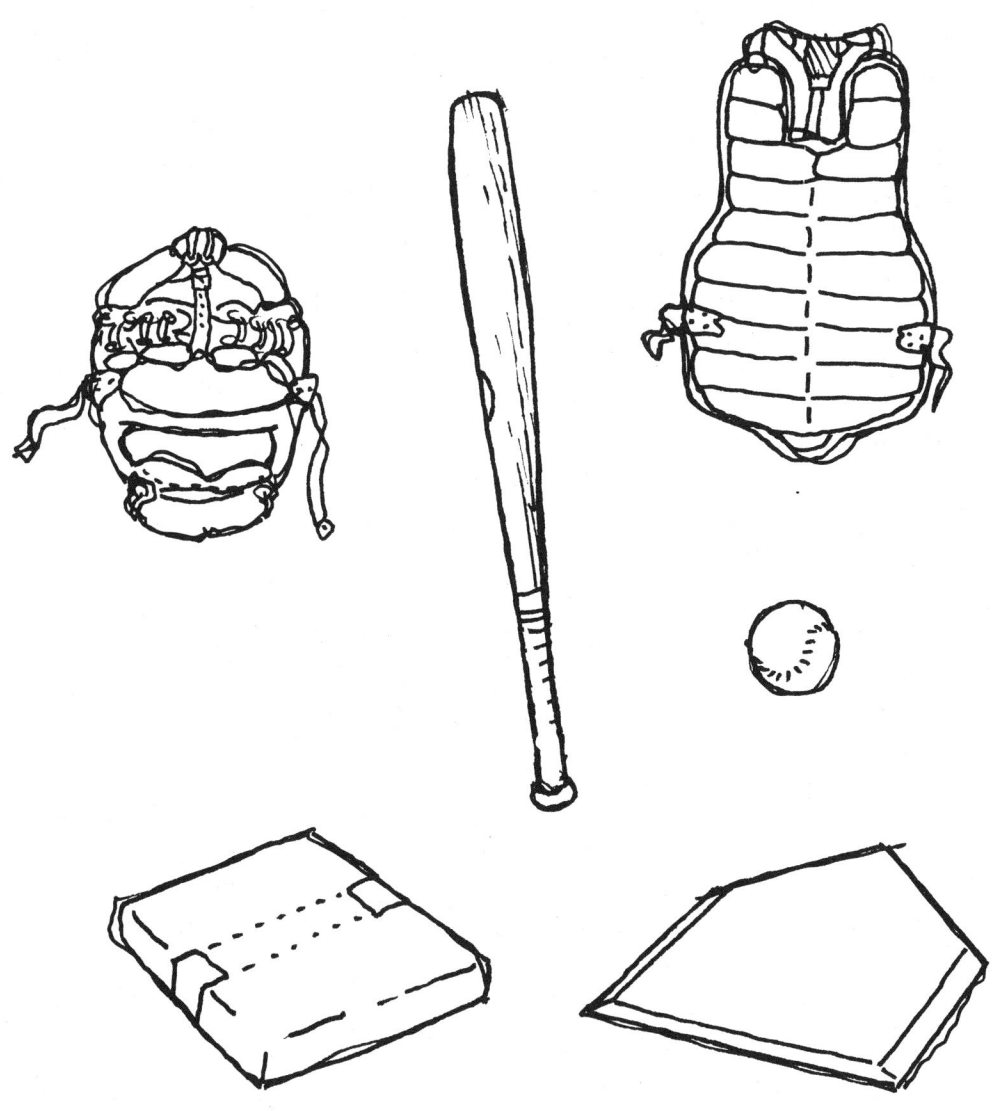

Some of the equipment used in softball (clockwise from the upper left): a catcher's mask, a bat, a catcher's chest protector, a softball, home plate and a base. **(Rule 3, Section 1–5)**

Most defensive players wear gloves; only the catcher and the first baseman may wear mitts. In fast pitch, both the catcher and the umpire wear a face mask and a chest protector.

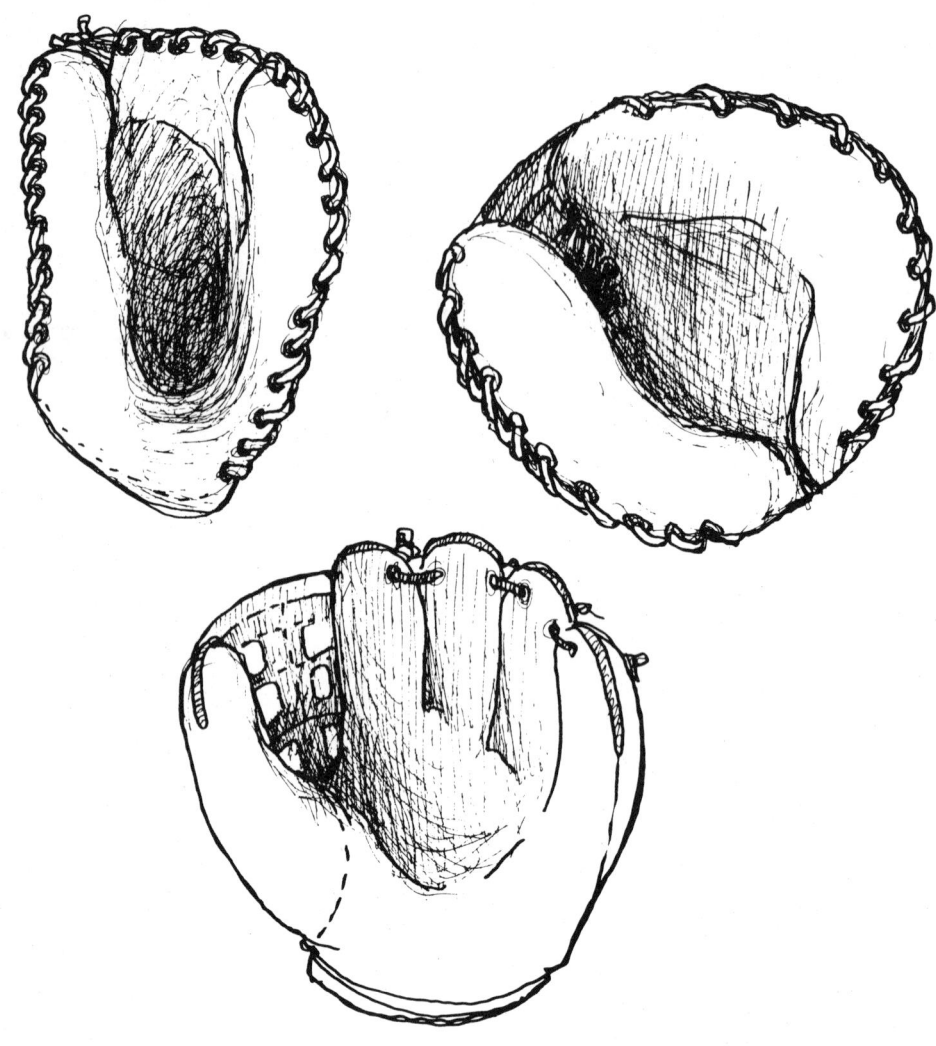

Three different kinds of mitts (clockwise from the top left): a first baseman's mitt, a catcher's mitt and a pitcher's or fielder's glove.

THE PITCHER

The pitcher stands in the center of the diamond and throws the ball for the batters to try to hit. The pitcher must follow certain rules to pitch properly. Failure to do so will result in an illegal pitch. In fast pitch, the penalty for an illegal pitch is a called ball for the batter and an extra base for any base runners. In slow pitch, a ball is called on the batter but the runners do not advance.

STANCE

Both the pitcher and the catcher must be in position before the pitcher is considered ready to pitch. **(Rule 6, Section 1c)** The catcher must be inside the catcher's box and the pitcher must stand squarely facing the batter.

In fast pitch, both feet must be in contact with the pitching rubber. In slow pitch softball, only one foot is required on the pitching rubber.

A fast pitch pitcher must begin with the ball held in both hands and both feet in contact with the pitcher's plate. He must come to a complete stop in this position for a least two and not more than twenty seconds before starting to pitch. **(Rule 6, Section 1a,b)**

Slow pitch rules are the same, except the pitcher is required to have only one foot on the pitching rubber and only one hand on the ball when he begins his motion.

THE DELIVERY

The pitcher may use any windup, but it is illegal to reverse the forward motion of the windup, or to continue the windup after the pitch is released. This is to prevent the pitcher from throwing "fake" pitches.

The ball must be thrown with a underhand motion, with the hand below the hip. The wrist may not be further from the body than the elbow. If the pitcher takes a step forward, it must be taken at the same time as the delivery of the ball. The pitcher's other foot must remain on the pitching rubber until the forward-stepping foot has touched the ground. **(Rule 6, Section 2)**

The delivery.

In slow pitch softball, the ball may not be delivered at excessive speed in the judgment of the umpire. Two offenses could result in the pitcher being removed from the mound. After leaving the pitcher's hand, the ball must arc at least three feet before crossing home plate. A pitch's maximum height off the ground in slow pitch is twelve feet. **(Rule 6, Section 3c)**

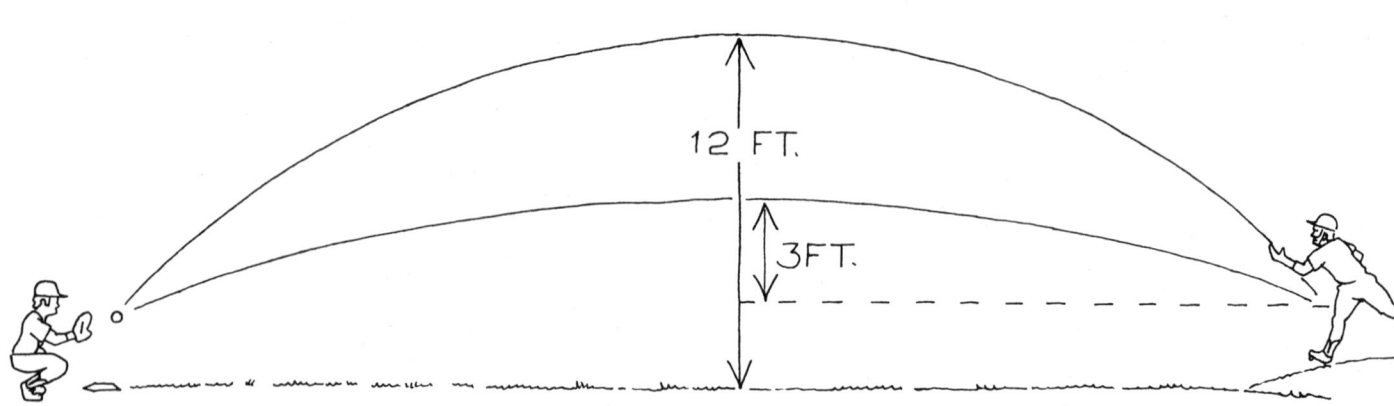

The maximum and minimum arc of a pitch in slow pitch softball.

INFRACTIONS

The pitcher may not stand in the pitching position unless he has the ball.

A pitch may not be deliberately rolled or bounced along the ground.

No foreign substance may be put on the ball, and the ball may not be intentionally defaced in any way. Not only will an illegal pitch be called, but the pitcher could be ejected from the game. **(Rule 6, Section 6)**

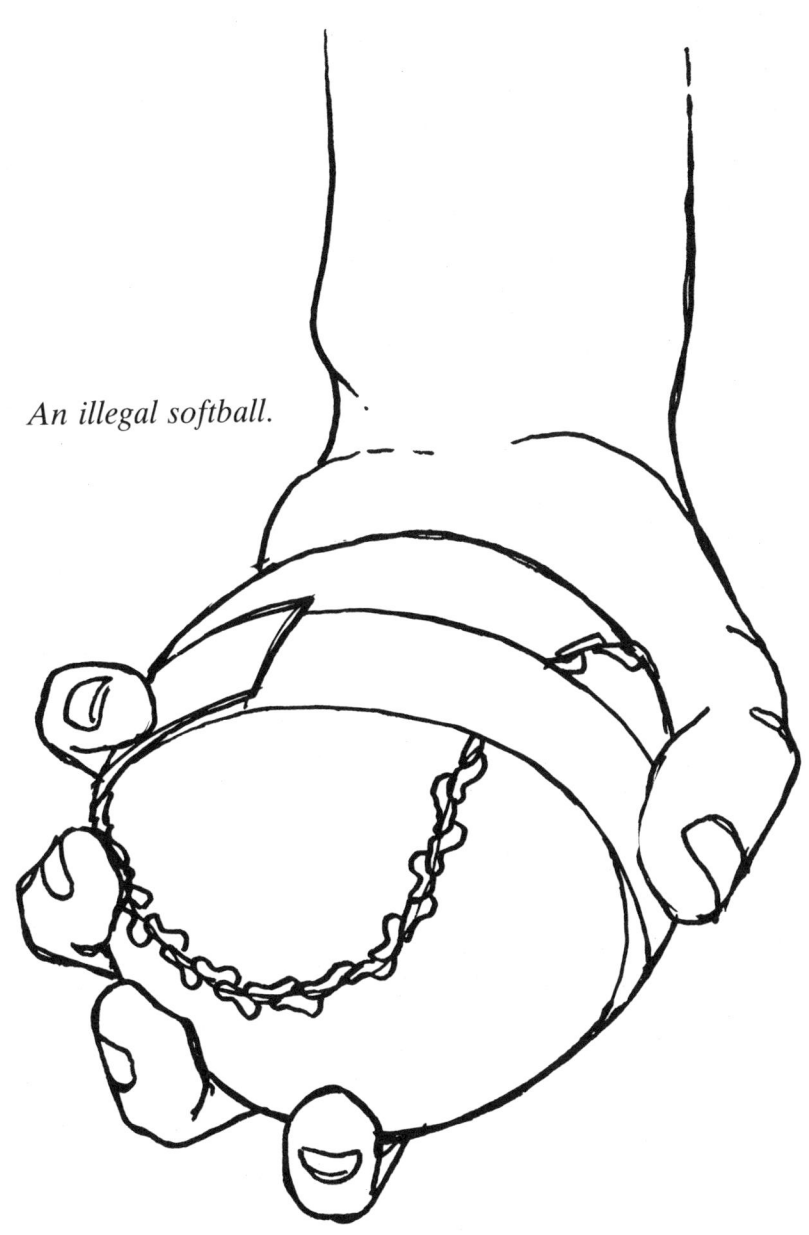

An illegal softball.

A pitch is illegal if the pitcher, after taking the pitching position, throws to a base while his foot is still in contact with the pitcher's plate. If he wishes to throw to a base he must step off the plate.

A "no-pitch" call by the umpire cancels any action resulting from a pitch. Some plays which result in a no-pitch are:

Pitching if the batter has not had time to get ready;

Pitching during a suspension of play;

The ball slipping loose during the pitcher's wind up (the base runners may advance in a fast pitch game);

A runner being called out for taking an illegal lead.

No pitch. The batter was not in the batter's box. **(Rule 6, Section 9b)**

DEAD BALL/LIVE BALL

The ball is dead when an illegal pitch is made and when most no-pitches are called. The base runners may not advance or be put out. However, in fast pitch, if a batter *hits* an illegal pitch and reaches first safely, and all the base runners advance at least one base, the play will be allowed to stand. This is what they would have been awarded anyway. In slow pitch, if the batter *swings* at an illegal pitch, the play stands regardless of the result.

THE BATTER

Each player must take his turn at bat in an established order. **(Rule 7, Section 2b)**

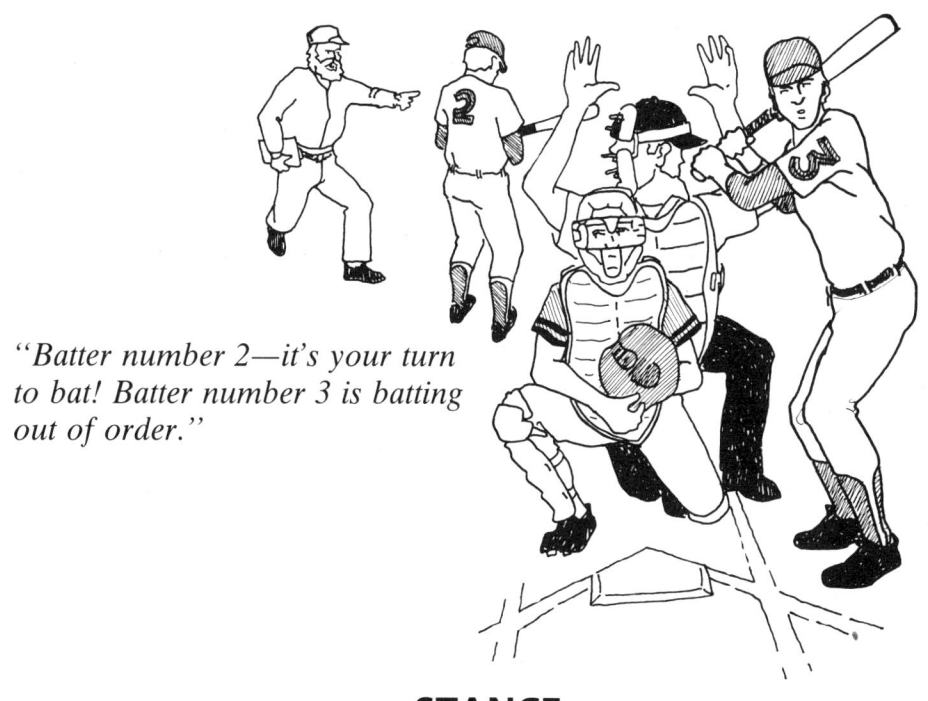

"Batter number 2—it's your turn to bat! Batter number 3 is batting out of order."

STANCE

The batter must stand with both feet on or within the lines of the batter's box, and must not touch home plate, **(Rule 7, Section 1a)**. The batter may not step in front of the catcher or switch batter's boxes when the pitcher is in the pitching position.

The batter must use a legal bat.

This batter is batting legally—both feet are in the batter's box.

STRIKES

Some of the Reasons Why a Strike Will Be Called

It is a strike if the batter swings at a pitched ball and misses it, even if it hits him. **(Rule 7, Section 6e)**

"Strike!"

It is a strike if a pitched ball enters the strike zone over home plate and the batter does not swing at it, even if it hits him. **(Rule 7, Section 6a)**

The Strike Zones

This pitch is in the strike zone. Even though it hits the batter, it is a strike.

It is a strike if the ball is hit into foul territory and is not caught on the fly, except if there are already two strikes on the batter. In that case, it is called a foul ball and the count on the batter remains at two strikes. **(Rule 7, Section 6d)**

"Foul ball!"

It is a strike if the ball is tipped directly back to the catcher, no higher than the batter's head, and the catcher is able to catch it or trap it against his body, as long as the ball hits his hands first. This is known as a "foul tip." Unlike other types of caught foul balls, a foul tip counts only for a strike, and *can* count for the third strike. **(Rule 7, Section 6c)**

The batter is not out unless this foul tip is his third strike.

It is a strike if the batter is hit with his own batted ball while he is still in the batter's box and has less than two strikes on him. **(Rule 7, Section 6f)**

BALLS

Some of the Reasons Why a Ball Will Be Called

The pitch is not swung at, and does not enter the strike zone.

The pitch not swung at hits home plate or touches the ground before entering the strike zone.

A ball is illegally pitched. In slow pitch a ball will be called if the batter does not swing at the pitch.

The pitcher fails to pitch within 20 seconds of taking the pitching position.

In slow pitch, the batter is hit on any part of the body outside the strike zone by a pitch he did not swing at. In fast pitch, he is awarded a base.

In slow pitch, any ball or strike results in a dead ball, and the runners may not try to advance.

In fast pitch, an uncaught foul ball or a batter being hit by a batted or pitched ball will result in a dead ball. However, a strike (even a third strike), a ball or a foul tip are all live balls, and the runners may try to advance.

WHEN THE BATTER IS OUT

Some Situations in Which a Batter Will Be Called Out

The batter will be called out if he fails to take his position within one minute after the umpire has called for the batter.

The batter is out if he steps in the batter's box with, or uses, an illegal bat.

The batter is out if he steps from one batter's box to the other when the pitcher is ready to pitch. **(Rule 7, Section 1b)**

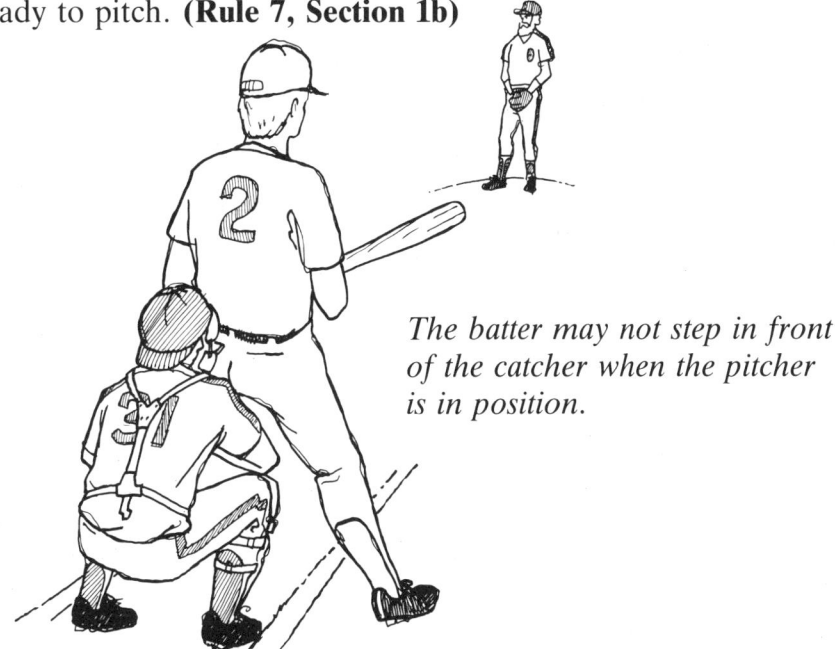

The batter may not step in front of the catcher when the pitcher is in position.

The batter is out if he has three strikes called against him, even if the ball hits the batter or is a foul tip. (Except when the "third strike rule" is in effect.) **(Rule 7, Section 11)**

"Strike three!"

The batter is out if he hits a fair fly ball which is caught by an opponent before it touches the ground.

The batter is out if he hits a foul fly ball which is caught by an opponent before it touches the ground.

This foul fly will be an out.

In fast pitch, the batter is out if he bunts foul with two strikes against him. In slow pitch, the batter is out if he bunts, fair or foul, no matter what the count.

Bunting in slow pitch softball is not allowed. This batter is out.

"Strike three, yer out!"

The batter will be called out if he intentionally hits the ball twice with the bat. The batter is not out if this is deemed unintentional. **(Rule 7, Section 5)**

The batter has intentionally hit the ball again with the bat. He is out.

The batter is out if his fair-hit ball touches him before being played by a fielder after he is out of the batter's box. **(Rule 8, Section 11k)**

"Yer out!"

The batter is out if he interferes with a play at the plate. If there are less than two outs, the runner coming from third is also out. **(Rule 8, Section 7h)**

The batter is interfering with a play at the plate.

The base runner is interfering with the fielder's play.

The batter is out if a preceding base runner intentionally interferes with, or fails to give the right of way to, a fielder who is trying to field the ball. The runner is also out. **(Rule 7, Section 4)**

The batter is out if, in the judgment of the umpire, a fielder intentionally drops a fly ball in order to create a force play. **(Rule 7, Section 11e)**

The fielder may not intentionally drop the ball to create a double play opportunity.

THE THIRD STRIKE RULE

The "third strike rule" is one time when three strikes do not make an out. This rule comes into effect when the catcher fails to catch a batter's third strike before the ball touches the ground, *and* there are less than two outs and first base is unoccupied by a runner, *or* if first base is occupied and there are two outs. These requirements prevent the catcher from

The catcher has dropped the third strike. Can the batter run?

dropping third strikes in order to create double play opportunities. If the catcher drops the third strike in these situations, the batter is not counted out and may try to run to first base. The batter is safe on first if he can beat the throw or avoid being tagged. Note: There is no third strike rule in slow pitch. **(Rule 7, Section 11h)**

The catcher has tagged the batter after dropping the third strike— the batter is now out.

THE INFIELD FLY RULE

The batter is out if he hits an infield fly and there are less than two outs and runners on first and second, or on first, second and third. An infield fly is a fair fly ball which might be caught with ordinary effort by an infielder. Line drives and bunts are not infield flies. This rule was designed to prevent the intentional dropping of fly balls to create double play situations. **(Rule 7, Section 11e)**

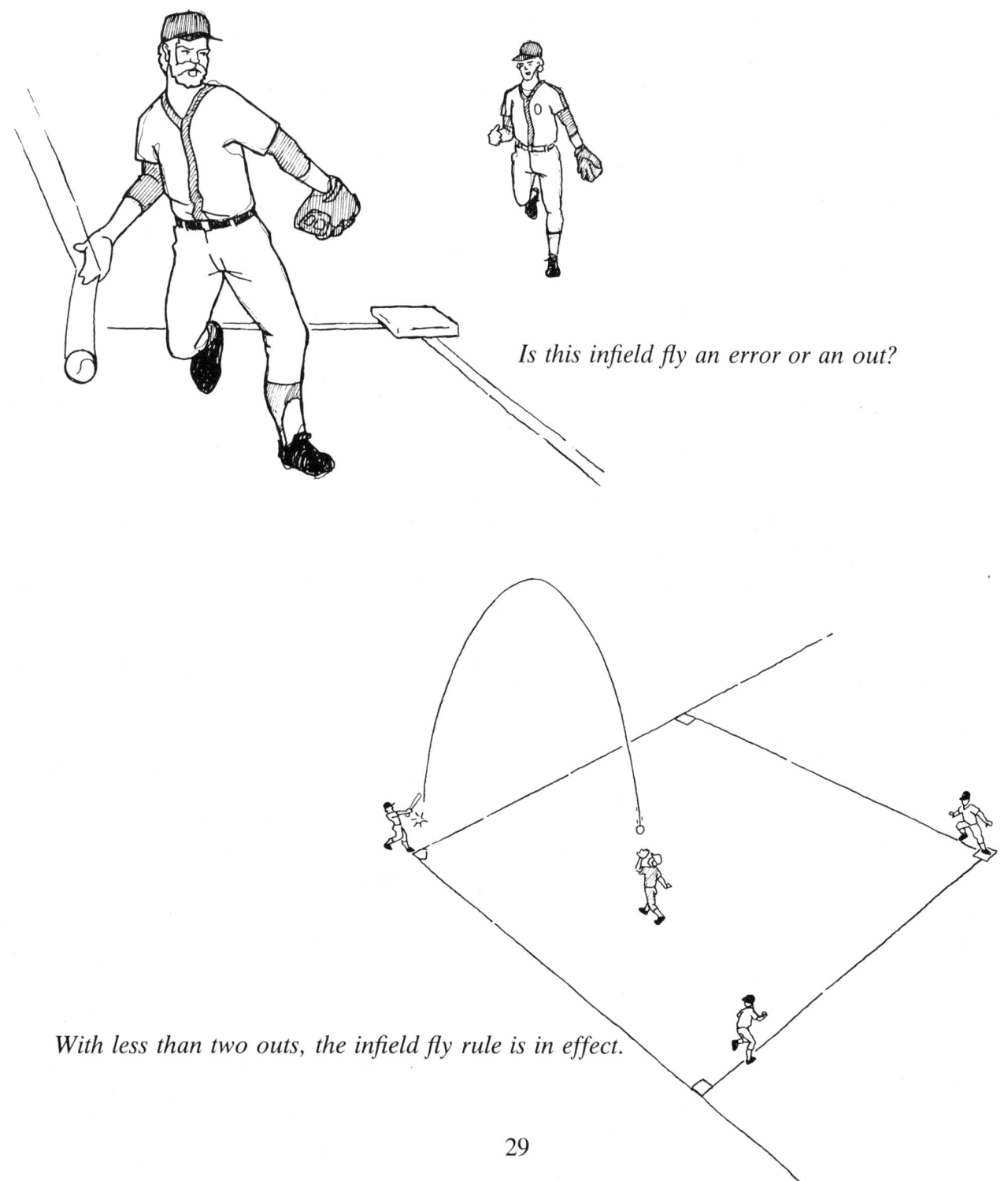

Is this infield fly an error or an out?

With less than two outs, the infield fly rule is in effect.

BASE RUNNING

Some General Rules

The runner must touch first, second, third and home bases in order to score a run.

The runner is safe.

A base runner acquires the right to a base by touching it before being put out. He is entitled to hold the base until he has legally touched the next base or is forced to vacate it by a runner following him. **(Rule 8, Section 1b)**

Runs may not be scored after the third out is made.

The third out has already been made—this runner does not score.

The runner at home does not score if this is the third out.

A run is not scored if a preceding runner is the third out on an appeal play.

A run is not scored if any other runner is forced out for the third out. **(Rule 5, Section 6b)**

What Happens to the Base Runners When the Batter Becomes a Base Runner

When a player at bat becomes a base runner, a runner at first base is forced to vacate that base. **(Rule 8, Section 1b,e)**

The batter has walked. The base runner at first base is forced to second base.

When the batter becomes a base runner, the base runner at second is forced to vacate that base if there is also a runner at first base.

When a player at bat becomes a base runner, the base runner at third base is forced to vacate that base if there are also runners at first and second.

Base runners are not forced to run if there are no runners immediately behind them, or if the runners behind them are not forced by the batter.

When a Batter Becomes a Base Runner

The batter becomes a base runner when he hits a fair ball.

A fair ball is a legally batted ball that lands in fair territory between first and third bases.

The batter has just hit the ball fairly and is now a base runner.

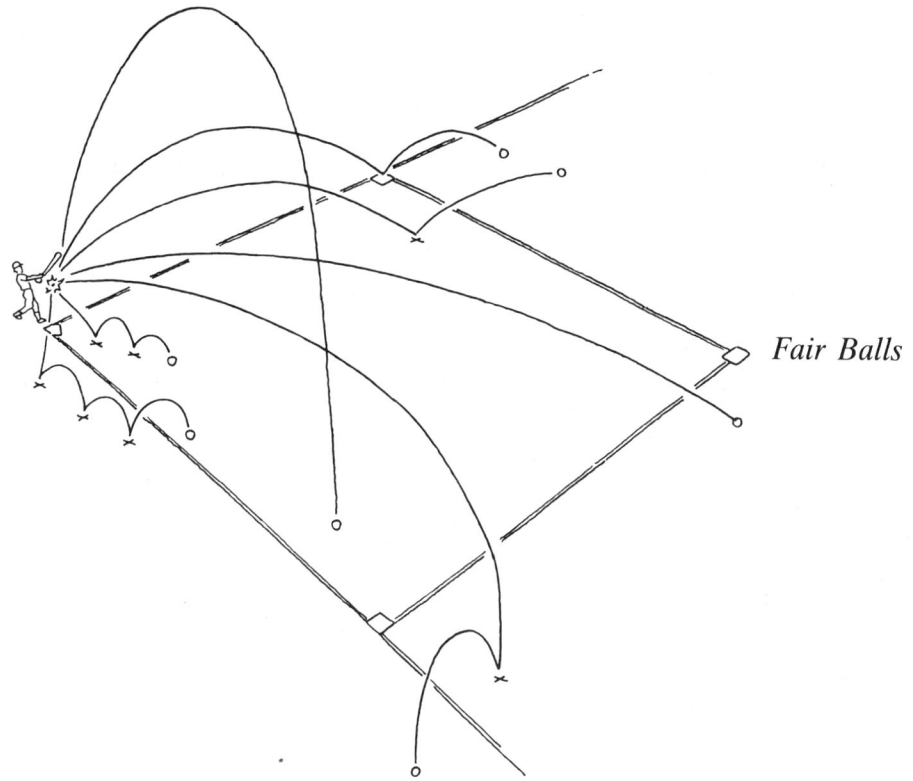

Fair Balls

A fair ball is a legally batted ball that bounces past first or third base in fair territory.

A fair ball is a legally batted ball that bounces on first or third base.

A fair ball is a legally batted ball that first falls fair between first or third base if it is a fly ball.

A fair ball is a legally batted ball that first falls fair beyond first or third if it is a fly ball.

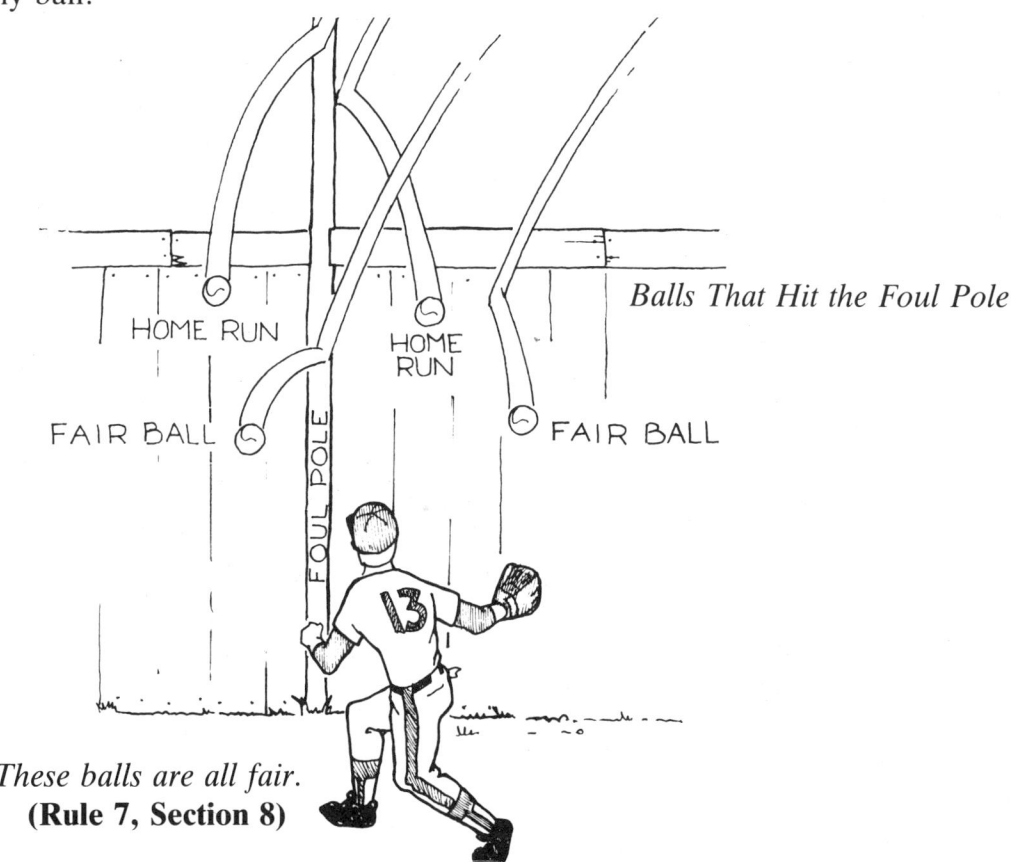

Balls That Hit the Foul Pole

These balls are all fair.
(Rule 7, Section 8)

This is a fair ball.

A fair ball remains fair and is in play if it strikes a base runner or an umpire *after* a fielder other than the pitcher has had a chance to play it. **(Rule 8, Section 2f)**

A ball is not fair if it strikes a base runner or an umpire *before* a fielder other than the pitcher has had a chance to play it. In that case it is a dead ball, and the batter will be awarded first base. The base runner hit is out and other runners not forced by the batter must return to their previous bases.

The ball is dead and the batter is awarded first base.

The ball has hit the base runner. Can the batter run?

The batter also becomes a base runner when the third strike rule is in effect and when he is awarded bases.

When the Batter Is Awarded One Base Without Jeopardy

The batter is awarded one base without jeopardy when four balls are called.

The batter is awarded one base without jeopardy when the catcher or any other fielder interferes with him. **(Rule 8, Section 2e)**

The catcher is interfering with the batter. The batter is allowed to take first base.

The batter is awarded one base without jeopardy when, in fast pitch, a pitched ball that the batter is not trying to swing at and is trying to avoid, hits him. In slow pitch, such a pitch is merely called a ball or a strike as the case may be. **(Rule 8, Section 2g)**

In fast pitch, the batter is awarded first base.

When the Batter Is Awarded Extra Bases Without Jeopardy

The batter is awarded *two* bases without jeopardy when a fielder touches a *thrown* ball with a detached glove, mask or part of his uniform.

The batter is awarded *three* bases without jeopardy when a fielder touches a *batted* ball with a detached glove, mask or piece of his uniform. **(Rule 8, Section 5f)**

The batter is awarded a home run when a fielder touches a ball that would have gone over the outfield fence with detached equipment, mask or uniform.

The fielder has touched a batted ball with his thrown glove.
The batter is awarded three bases.

When a Base Runner May Legally Leave His Base

In slow pitch, a base runner may legally leave his base when a pitched ball crosses home plate.

In fast pitch, a base runner may legally leave his base when a pitched ball leaves the pitcher's hand. **(Rule 8, Section 3a)**

This lead-off is legal in fast pitch. Is it legal in slow pitch?

In slow pitch, although the batter may leave when the ball crosses home plate, the ball is dead on every strike or ball. Unlike in fast pitch, runners may not advance to the next base unless the ball is batted.

A runner who has begun a legal advance cannot be stopped by the pitcher getting ready to pitch with the ball in his hand. The runner must, however, either proceed to the next base or return to the one he is entitled to hold. **(Rule 8, Section 9i)**

The runner continues to second base.

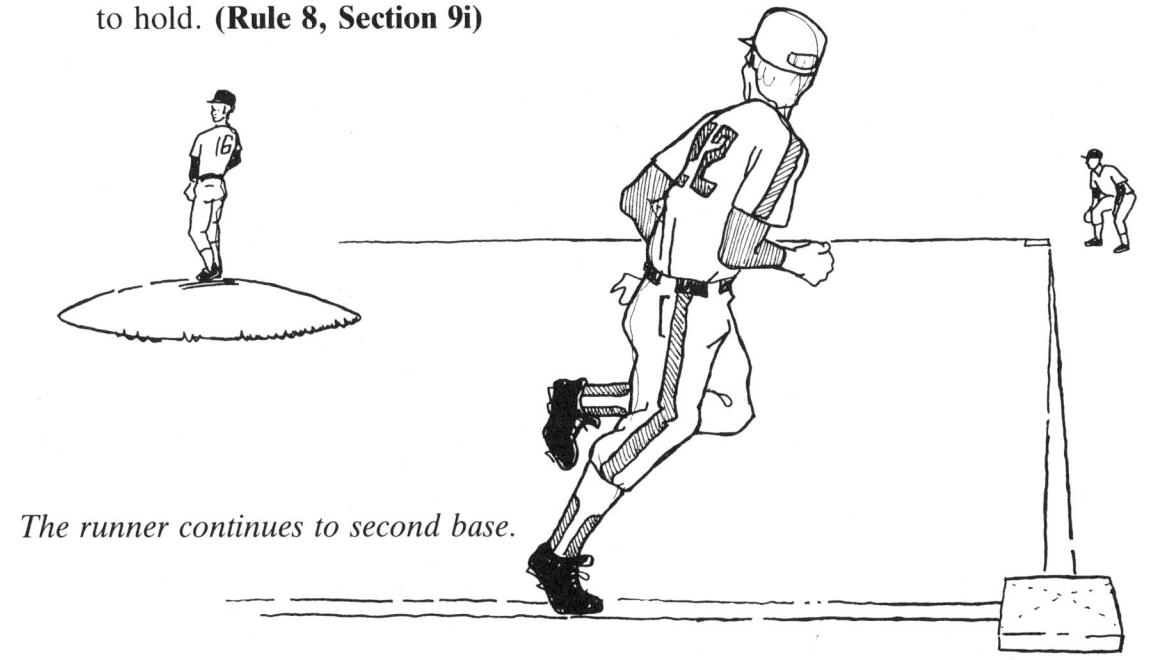

The runner is off!

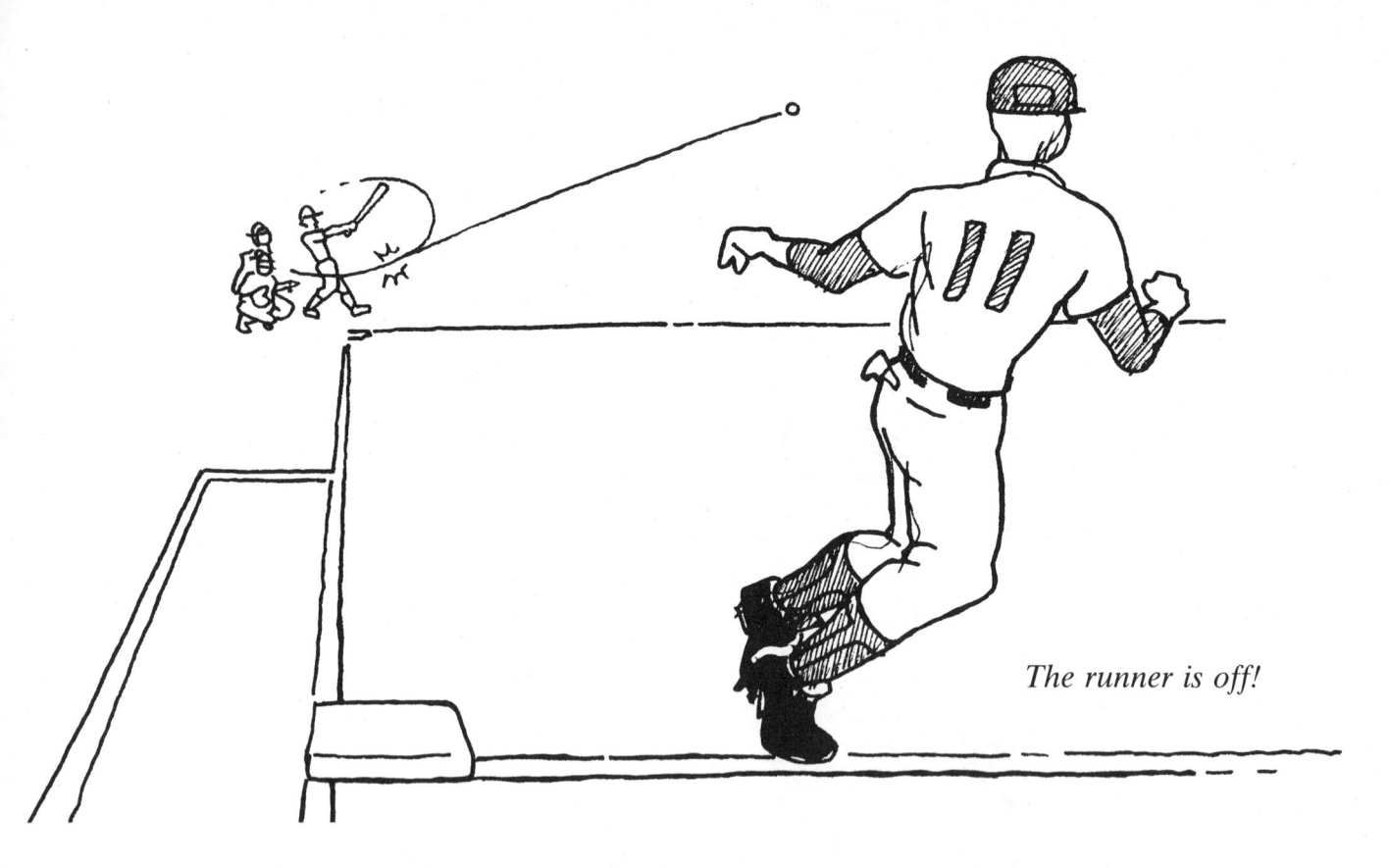

When Base Runners May Try for More Bases at Their Own Risk

Base runners may try for more bases at their own risk when the ball is hit into fair territory.

Base runners may try for more bases at their own risk when a legally caught fly ball, fair or foul, is first touched. **(Rule 8, Section 3d)**

Once a foul ball is touched, a base runner can run.

Base runners may try for more bases at their own risk when the ball is overthrown, including a wild pitch, but not if thrown out of the park or into unplayable territory. **(Rule 8, Section 3b)**

An overthrown ball—the base runner is free to run.

A wild pitch—the runner is free to advance.

Some of the Times a Base Runner Is Given the Right to Advance *One* Base Without Risk

A base runner is given the right to advance one base without risk when he is forced to because a base is awarded to the batter.

A base runner is given the right to advance one base without risk when a wild pitch goes into the stands or lodges in the backstop. **(Rule 8, Section 5c)**

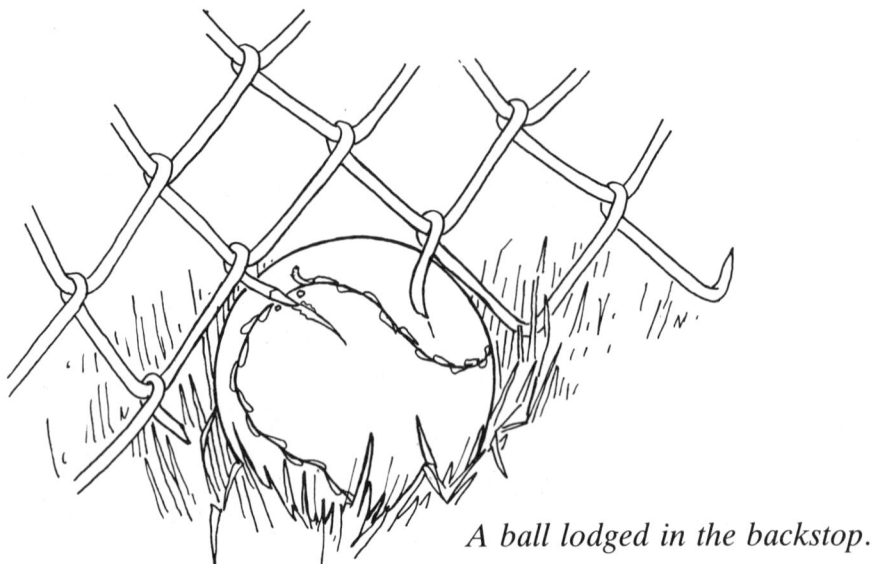

A ball lodged in the backstop.

A base runner is given the right to advance one base without risk when a legally caught ball is carried into dead ball territory (for example, if the player making the catch falls into the dugout).

A base runner is given the right to advance one base without risk when a fielder who is not trying to field the ball interferes with the base runner. In this case, the runner could be awarded more than one base. **(Rule 8, Section 5b)**

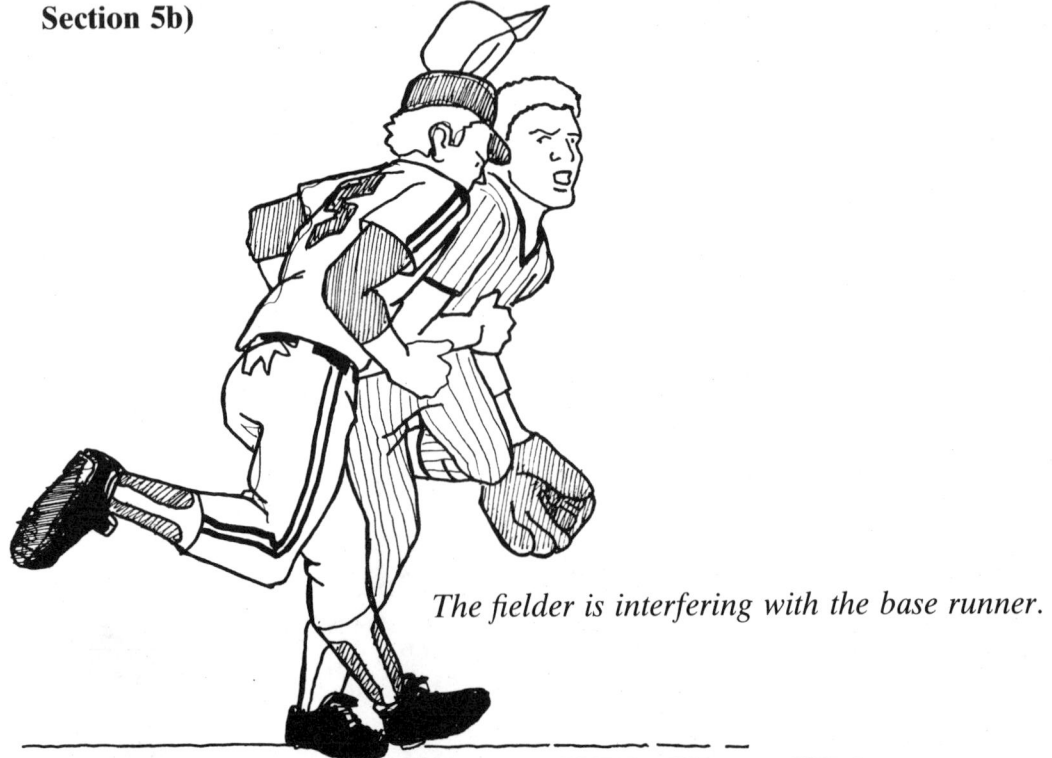

The fielder is interfering with the base runner.

A base runner is given the right to advance one base without risk when, in fast pitch, the pitcher makes an illegal pitch.

Some of the Times a Base Runner Is Given the Right to Advance *Two* **Bases Without Risk**

A base runner is given the right to advance two bases without risk when a fair ball is hit over the fence on an undersized playing field. **(Rule 8, Section 5h)**

The base runners are allowed to advance only two bases when a ball is hit out of the park on an undersized field.

A base runner is given the right to advance two bases without risk when a fair ball bounds or rolls into unplayable territory (the famous "ground-rule double").

A base runner is given the right to advance two bases without risk when a thrown ball is illegally played.

Base runners advance two bases if an overthrow by an *infielder* lands in unplayable territory. If an overthrow by an *outfielder* is unplayable, base runners are given two bases from where they were at the time of the throw. **(Rule 8, Section 5g)**

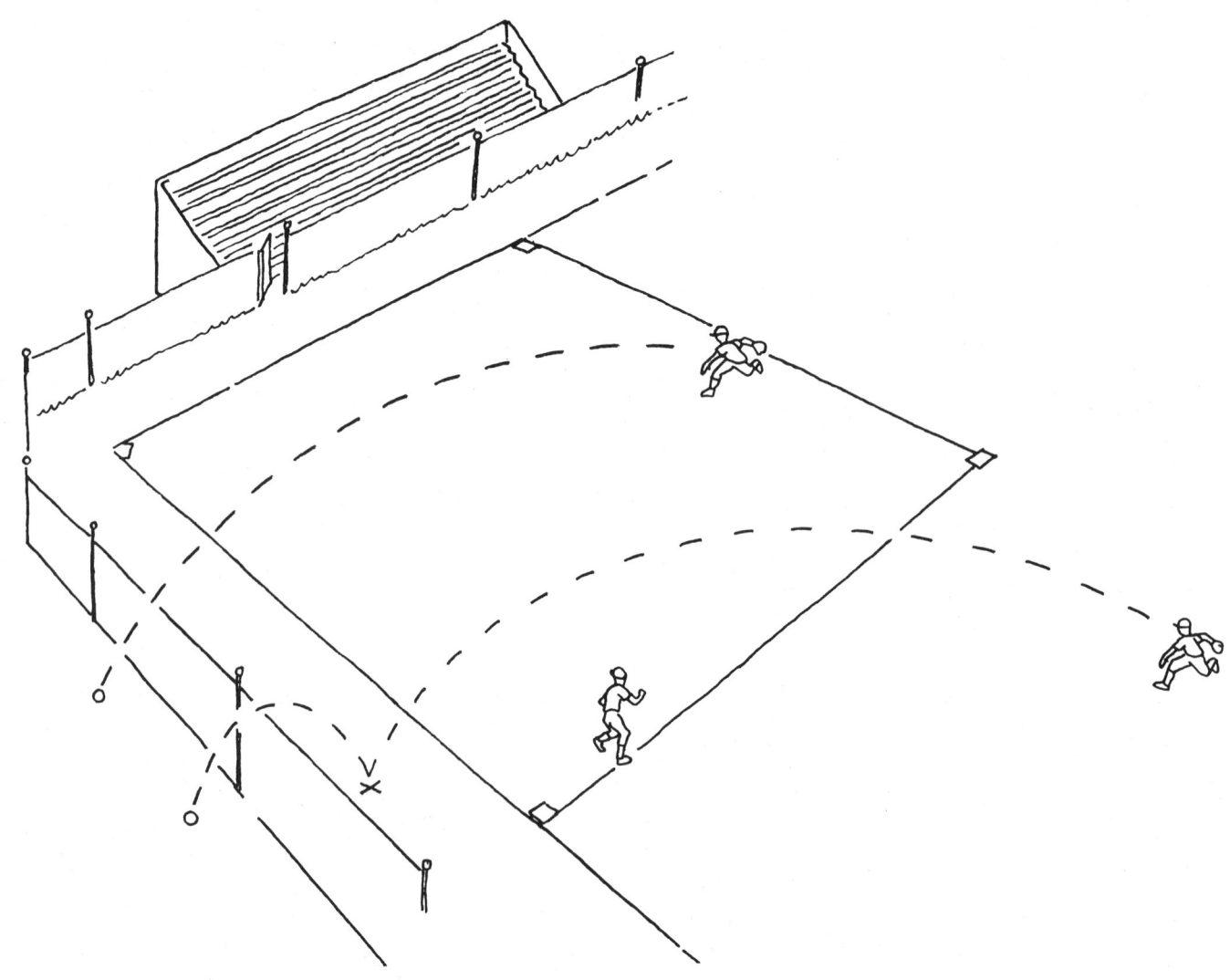

The base runner is awarded two extra bases.

Some of the Times a Base Runner May Advance Further Without Risk

Base runners are given the right to advance three bases without risk if a fielder touches a batted ball with a detached glove, mask or part of his uniform. The base runner advances three bases, and may advance home without risk if the ball would have gone over the fence for a home run. **(Rule 8, Section 5f)**

Base runners may advance to home without jeopardy when a fair fly ball is hit into unplayable territory over the outfield fence. The batter advances four bases—in other words, a home run. **(Rule 8, Section 5h)**

The batter has been hit by the pitcher. The base runner must return to third.

When a Runner Must Return to Base

A runner must return to base when a batter or base runner is called out for interference with the ball or a fielder.

A base runner must return to base when the batter is hit by a pitched ball, whether it's a strike or a ball, even if the runner is going to be advanced by the batter being awarded a base.

The runner must return to base when an infield fly is called. **(Rule 6, Section 6f)**

The runner must return to base when a ball is illegally batted.

The runner must return to base if the ball hits the umpire before a defensive player other than the pitcher has had a chance to play it.

In slow pitch, a runner must return to base when a pitched ball is not hit.

WHEN THE BASE RUNNER IS OUT

A base runner will not be called out for overrunning first base, as long as he returns directly to the base.

Some of the Reasons a Base Runner Will Be Called Out
A base runner will be called out if a fielder holding the ball touches the base to which the runner is forced before the runner does. **(Rule 8, Section 8c)**

The runner is out.

"Gotcha!"

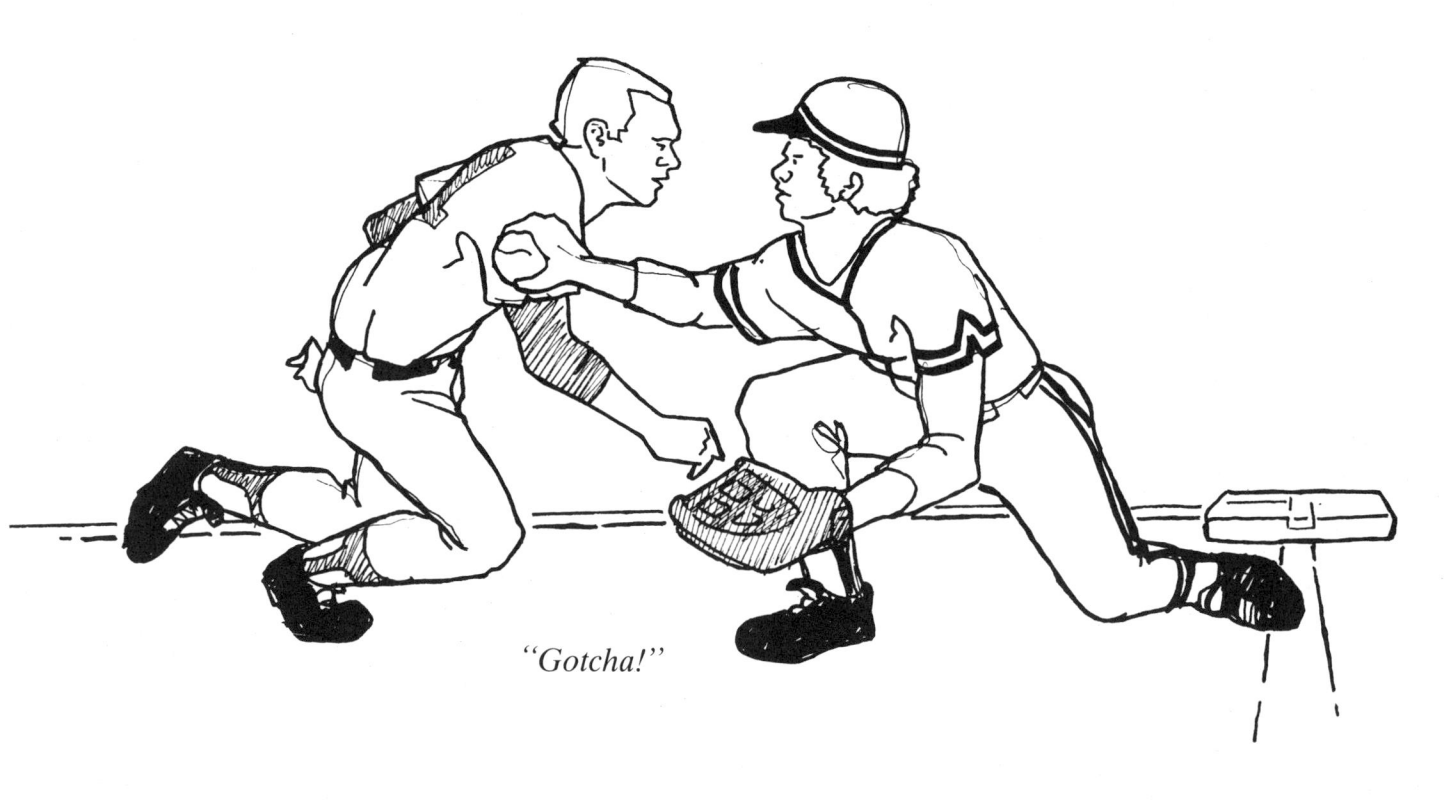

If the base runner is tagged with the ball by a fielder while he is standing off the base to which he is entitled. For example:

when trying for the next base;

when returning to base after a fair fly ball has been caught;

when oversliding second or third base, or improperly overrunning first by moving toward second.

The runner has overslid third base.

The runner is out.

The base runner will be called out if he leaves base early or fails to return to base when the pitcher is preparing to pitch. **(Rule 8, Section 8)**

The runner is out if he runs outside the base path to avoid being tagged. He is not out if he leaves the base path to yield the right of way to a fielder. **(Rule 8, Section 8a, 9a)**

This runner is running outside the base path.

"That's interference."

The base runner will be called out if he intentionally interferes with, or fails to yield the right of way to, a fielder playing the ball. If this interference is an obvious attempt to break up a double play, the runner immediately following will also be out. **(Rule 8, Section 8j)**

Interference—both runners are out.

A runner from third base will be out if the batter, or his teammates, interferes with the play at the plate. If there are less than two outs the batter will also be called out.

If teammates gather around a base to break up a play the runner will be out. **(Rule 8, Section 8p)**

The manager is interfering with the play. The runner is out.

"Darn—that line drive hit me. I'm out."

If he is struck by a fair ball before it passes a fielder other than the pitcher the runner is out. **(Rule 8, Section 8k)**

If the ball is interfered with by a coach the runner is out. A runner is out if he is bodily assisted by a coach.

"You're not allowed to pass me."

If, while on the base path, he passes another runner who is not out, the first runner is out. **(Rule 8, Section 8e)**

If two base runners occupy the same base at the same time, and it is not a force play, the runner arriving last is tagged out. **(Rule 8, Section 1b,e)**

"You're out!"

If a judgment is made against a base runner on an appeal play, the runner is out. **(Rule 8, Section 8g)**

An appeal play. The umpire must make a ruling.

A runner cannot be tagged out for failure to be in contact with a dislodged base, provided the runner does not begin to try for the next base, and should be in the approximate spot where the base would be. **(Rule 8, Section 8h)**

This runner has overrun first base and is heading toward second. He can be tagged out.

APPEAL PLAYS

An appeal play is made to the umpire by the defensive team by claiming that a violation of the rules has occurred. The appeal must be made by a defensive player before the next pitch is made to a batter. The ball may be in play during an appeal and ruling.

Some Common Appeal Plays

A runner may be called out if he overslides home plate or misses the plate and is tagged with the ball before he can return to touch the plate. **(Rule 8, Section 8i)**

The runner has missed home plate.

The runner will be out if an appeal is made.

The runner may be called out if he misses a base. The defensive player then must tag the runner or the base with the ball before the runner returns. It is important to remember that if the runner misses a base, it does not affect the status or progress of the following runners unless the runner's error results in the third out. **(Rule 8, Section 8g,i)** If the runner realizes his mistake and tries to return, he must return to the base along the base path. The runner may not return if other runners have advanced to or past that base or if he has already crossed home plate. **(Rule 8, Section 8g)**

A runner may be called out if he fails to return to first base immediately after overrunning or oversliding and the ball has been caught by the first baseman after the runner has crossed the base. The runner may pivot left toward second base but may not make a move to advance.

This runner returned to third base after missing it moments before.

BATTING OUT OF TURN

The defensive team may make an appeal play if a batter bats out of turn. **(Rule 7, Section 2)**

Batter number 12 was batting out of turn.

All batting and fielding substitutions must be reported to the umpire. The new player must take the place in the batting order of the player he replaces.

If a batter bats out of turn, and the error is noticed, the proper batter must take over with the existing ball and strike count.

If the error is not noticed until the incorrect batter has finished his turn at bat, the correct batter who missed his turn is out and any runs or bases made do not count. If the error is not noticed and the pitcher pitches to the next batter without an appeal being made, the game continues and the batter who missed his turn is not out.

UMPIRES

The umpire has complete charge and authority once the game has started and can make decisions on situations not specifically covered in the rules.

When there is one umpire, he should position himself in any part of the field that, in his judgment, will best enable him to carry out his duties. **(Rule 10, Section 4)**

A player cannot question an umpire's judgment.

Points of the rules may be questioned, but not the umpire's judgment.

"Stop the game!"

It is the umpire's duty to stop the game when it is no longer safe to play. **(Rule 10, Section 8)**

If there is more than one umpire calling the game, the plate umpire has full charge of, and is responsible for, the proper conduct of the game. The base umpire(s) should assist the plate umpire in every way, as outlined in the umpires manual.

OFFICIAL SOFTBALL PLAYING RULES

Copyright by the Amateur Softball Association of America REVISED 1987

"Permission to reprint THE OFFICIAL PLAYING RULES has been granted by THE AMATEUR SOFTBALL ASSOCIATION OF AMERICA"

> Wherever, in this rule book, "he" or "him" or their related pronouns may appear either as words or as parts of words, they have been used for literary purposes and are meant in their generic sense (i.e., to include all humankind or both female and male sexes).

New rules have been italicized in each section. All plays are also italicized whether pertaining to new rules or old.
► NOT ITALICIZED WITH THIS MARKING MEANS CHANGE IN WORDING FOR CLARIFICATION ONLY. NO CHANGE IS MADE IN THE RULE.

RULE 1. DEFINITIONS

Sec. 1. ALTERED BAT. A bat is considered altered when the physical structure of a legal bat has been changed. Examples of altering a bat are: replacing the handle of a metal bat with a wooden or other type handle, inserting material inside the bat, applying excessive tape (more than two layers) to the bat grip, or painting a bat at the top or bottom for other than identification purposes. Replacing the grip with another legal grip is not considered altering the bat. A "flare or cone" grip attached to the bat is considered an altered bat.

PLAY —   B1 hits two-base hit with an aluminum bat containing a wooden handle. RULING — The ball is dead, batter is out, and baserunners may not advance. The batter is ejected for using an altered bat.

►**Sec. 2. APPEAL PLAY.** An appeal play is a play in which an umpire cannot make a decision until requested by a manager, coach or player. The appeal must be made before the next legal or illegal pitch, or before the defensive team has left the field. The defensive team has "left the field" when the pitcher and all infielders have clearly left their normal fielding positions and have left fair territory on their way to the bench or dugout area.

PLAY —   With R1 on first, B2 hits a double. R1 goes to third but fails to touch second. Umpire observes this but no appeal is made. B2 goes to second. Since no appeal was made, is the procedure the same as if R1 had touched second? RULING — Yes.

Sec. 3. BASE ON BALLS. A base on balls permits a batter to gain first base without liability to be put out and is awarded to a batter by the umpire when four pitches are judged to be balls.

Sec. 4. BASE PATH. A base path is an imaginary line three feet (0.91 m) on either side of a direct line between the bases.

Sec. 5. BASERUNNER. A baserunner is a player of the team at bat who has finished his turn at bat, reached first base, and has not yet been put out.

Sec. 6. BATTED BALL. A batted ball is any ball that hits the bat or is hit by the bat and lands either in fair or foul territory. No intention to hit the ball is necessary.

Sec. 7. BATTER'S BOX. The batter's box is the area to which the batter is restricted while in position with the intention of helping his team to obtain runs. The lines are considered as being within the batter's box. Prior to the pitch, the batter must have both feet entirely within the lines of the batter's box.

Sec. 8. BATTER-BASERUNNER. A batter-baserunner is a player who has finished his turn at bat but has not yet been put out or touched first base.

Sec. 9. BATTING ORDER. The batting order is the official listing of offensive players in the order in which members of that team must come to bat. When the lineup card is submitted, it shall also include each player's position.

►**Sec. 10. BLOCKED BALL.** A blocked ball is a batted or thrown ball that is touched, stopped or handled by a person not engaged in the game, or which touches any object that is not part of the official equipment or official playing area.
EFFECT — The ball is dead. If a fielder, other than the pitcher causing a blocked ball (and interference), the player being played on is out. *If no apparent play is obvious, all runners will return to last base touched at the time of the dead ball declaration.* See Rule 8, Section 5g for enforcement.

PLAY —   A blocked ball is called when (a) it hits the coach, (b) it strikes a spectator. RULING — (a) No, (b) Yes.

Sec. 11. BUNT. A bunt is a legally tapped ball not swung at, but intentionally met with the bat and tapped slowly within the infield.

Sec. 12. CATCH. A catch is a legally caught ball which occurs when the fielder catches a batted or thrown ball with his hands or glove. If the ball is merely held in the fielder's arms or prevented from dropping to the ground by some part of the fielder's body or clothing, the catch is not completed until the ball is in the grasp of the fielder's hands or glove. It is not a catch if a fielder, immediately after he contacts the ball, collides with another player or wall, or falls to the ground and drops the ball as a result of the collision or falling to the ground. In establishing a valid catch, the fielder shall hold the ball long enough to prove he has complete control of the ball and that his release of the ball is voluntary and intentional. If a player drops the ball after reaching into his glove to remove the ball or while in the act of throwing the ball, it is a valid catch.

PLAY (1) —   A legal catch is when a fielder holds the ball in his (a) hand, (b) under his arm, (c) cap, (d) glove. RULING — (a) Yes, (b) No, (c) No, (d) Yes.

PLAY (2) —   B1 hits line drive which, after passing F3, strikes the umpire while the ball is over fair ground. The ball ricochets and is fielded by F4 while still in flight. RULING — This is not a catch. The ball, which strikes anything other than a defensive player while it is in flight, is ruled the same as if it struck the ground. B1 would have to be thrown out or tagged out.

PLAY (3) —   F3 and F4 both attempt to field a fly ball. Before touching the ground, the ball strikes F4 on the head and, while still in the air (hasn't touched the ground), is caught by F3. RULING — This is a legally caught fly ball.

PLAY (4) —   B1 hits fly to F8. F8 gets the ball in his hands but drops it (a) when he falls to the ground and rolls over, or (b) when he collides with a fielder or a wall, or (c) when he starts to throw to the infield. RULING — In (a) and (b) it is not a catch. In (c), it is a legal catch if ball was held long enough for F8 to regain his balance but then drops it in a motion associated with an intended throw.

Sec. 13. CATCHER'S BOX. The catcher's box is that area within which the catcher must stand while and until:
a. (FP ONLY) The pitch is released. The lines are to be considered within the catcher's box.
b. (SP ONLY) The pitched ball is batted or reaches the catcher's box. The lines are to be considered within the catcher's box, AND ALL PARTS OF THE CATCHER'S BODY AND/OR EQUIPMENT MUST BE WITHIN THE CATCHER'S BOX UNTIL THE PITCHED BALL IS BATTED OR REACHES THE CATCHER'S BOX.
EFFECT — Sec. 13b: An illegal pitch is called, providing the batter does not swing.

NOTE: For catcher's box dimensions see Rule 2, Sec 4d.

Sec. 14. CHARGED CONFERENCE. A charged conference takes place when:
a. (Defensive Conference) The defensive team requests a suspension of play for any reason and a representative (not in the field) of the defensive team enters the playing field and gives the umpire cause to believe that he has delivered a message (by any means) to the pitcher.
b. (Offensive Conference) The offensive team requests a suspension of play to allow the manager or other team representatives to confer with the batter or baserunner. Refer to Rule 5, Section 9.

Sec. 15. CHOPPED BALL. (SP ONLY) A chopped hit ball is one at which the batter strikes downward with a chopping motion.

Sec. 16. COACH. A coach is a member of the team at bat who takes his place within the coach's box on the field to direct the players of his team in running the bases. Two coaches are allowed. One coach can have in his possession in the coach's box a scorebook, pen or pencil, and an indicator, which shall be used for scorekeeping or record keeping purposes only.

Sec. 17. DEAD BALL. The ball is not in play and is not considered in play again until the pitcher has the ball in his possession, is within eight feet (2.44 m) of the pitcher's plate, and the plate umpire has called "play ball." A dead ball line is considered in play. Refer to Rule 1, Section 49 for "Play Ball."

Sec. 18. DEFENSIVE TEAM. The defensive team is the team in the field.

Sec. 19. DISLODGED BASE. A dislodged base is a base removed from its proper position.

Sec. 20. DOUBLE PLAY. A double play is a play by the defense resulting in two offensive players being legally put out as a result of continuous action.

Sec. 21. FAIR BALL. A fair ball is a batted ball that:
a. Settles or is touched on fair territory between home and first base or between home and third base.
b. Bounds past first or third base on or over fair territory.
c. While on or over fair territory, touches the person, attached equipment or clothing of a player or an umpire.
d. Touches first, second or third base.
e. First falls or is first touched on or over fair territory beyond first, second or third base.
f. While over fair territory, passes out of the playing field beyond the outfield fence.

NOTE: A fair fly shall be judged according to the relative position of the ball and

61

the foul line, including the foul pole, and not as to whether the fielder is on fair or foul territory at the time he touches the ball. It does not matter whether the ball first touches fair or foul territory, as long as it does not touch anything foreign to the natural ground in foul territory and complies with all other aspects of a fair ball.

PLAY (1) — *Batted ball settles on home plate.* RULING — *Fair Ball.*

PLAY (2) — *Batted ball first hits foul ground and, without touching any foreign object, rolls into fair territory between first and home or third and home, where it settles.* RULING — *Fair Ball.*

Sec. 22. FAIR TERRITORY. Fair territory is that part of the playing field within and including the first and third base foul lines from home base to the bottom of the extreme playing field fence and perpendicularly upward.

Sec. 23. FAKE TAG. A form of obstruction which impedes the progress of a runner. The runner does not have to stop or slide, only slow down, to be considered a fake tag. NOTE: Under Rule 8, Sec. 5b(3), a player may be removed from the game for a fake tag infraction.

Sec. 24. FIELDER. A fielder is any player of the team in the field.

Sec. 25. FLY BALL. A fly ball is any ball batted into the air.

Sec. 26. FORCE-OUT. A force-out is an out which can be made only when a baserunner loses the right to the base he is occupying because the batter becomes a batter-baserunner, and before the batter-baserunner or a succeeding baserunner has been put out.

▶NOTE: If the forced runner, after touching the next base, retreats for any reason towards the base he had last occupied, the force play is reinstated, and he can again be put out if the defense tags the base to which he is forced.

PLAY (1) — *R1 is on first base. B2 hits sharp grounder to F3, who first touches first base then touches R1, who is still on first base.* RULING — *Only B2 is out. F3's act eliminated the force, thereby permitting R1 to remain on first.*

PLAY (2) — *R1 on 1B when B2 hits a short fly ball to left field. R1 goes approximately 15 feet off base waiting to see if the ball will be caught. B2 rounds 1B and passes R1 and the umpires calls B2 out. The ball drops in front of a base hit. R1 advances to 2B and F4 with the ball tags 2B before R1 slides into the base.* RULING: *The force out is removed when B2 passes R1 and therefore F4 had to tag R1. The runner is safe sliding into 2B if he was not tagged.*

Sec. 27. FOUL BALL. A foul ball is a batted ball that:
a. Settles on foul territory between home and first base, or between home and third base.
b. Bounds past first or third base over foul territory.
c. While on or over foul territory, touches the person, attached equipment, or clothing of a player or an umpire, or any object foreign to the natural ground.
d. First falls or is first touched over foul territory beyond first or third base.
e. Touches the batter while the ball is within the batter's box.
f. Hits the bat in the batter's hand while within the batter's box.

NOTE: A foul fly shall be judged according to the relative position of the ball and the foul line, including the foul pole, and not as to whether the fielder is on foul or fair territory at the time he touches the ball.

PLAY (1) — *A fair ball is called when (a) the ball hits the bag and deflects into foul territory, (b) the ball bounds from the infield over the base and lands in foul territory, (c) the ball lands within the confines of the infield and rolls foul without being touched by a fielder.* RULING — *(a) Correct, (b) Correct, (c) False.*

PLAY (2) — *Bat of B1 breaks into pieces as a result of hitting a pitch. The batted ball, bounding on foul territory in direction of third base, then hits the barrel of the bat causing the ball to roll into fair territory in front of third base. F5 fields the ball and throws it to F3, who tags first base before B1 reaches it.* RULING — *Foul ball, but B1 is not out for hitting ball a second time.*

Sec. 28. FOUL TIP. A foul tip is a batted ball which goes directly from the bat, not higher than the batter's head, to the catcher's hands and is legally caught by the catcher.

NOTE: It is not a foul tip unless caught; and any foul tip that is caught, is a strike. In fast pitch the ball is in play. In slow pitch the ball is dead. It is not a catch if it is a rebound, unless the ball first touched the catcher's hand or glove.

PLAY (1) — *Ball goes directly from bat and rebounds from protector (a) of F2 after having touched his glove, (b) of F2 without first having touched his glove, (c) of umpire after having first touched glove of F2, (d) of umpire without first having touched glove of F2 and is held.* RULING — *In (a), it is a foul tip and a strike. In (b), (c) and (d), it is a foul with ball becoming dead when it touched F2 in (b) or umpire in (c) and (d).*

PLAY (2) — *(FP ONLY) With R1 on second, B2 hits foul tip. May R1 advance without retouching second? Also, does it make any difference if the catcher drops the batted ball?* RULING — *A foul tip is the same as any strike, hence R1 may advance without retouching. If batted ball is not caught, it is not a foul tip and is ruled a foul ball.*

Sec. 29. HELMET. A helmet shall be the type which has safety features equal to or greater than those provided by the full plastic cap with padding on the inside. Extended ear flaps are optional. The liner type helmet does not meet the rules specification.

Sec. 30. HOME TEAM. The home team is the team on whose grounds the game is played. If the game is played on neutral ground, the home team shall be designated by mutual agreement or by a flip of a coin.

Sec. 31. ILLEGAL BAT. An illegal bat is one that does not meet the requirements of Rule 3, Section 1.

PLAY — *B1 hits a double to centerfield. Umpire notices bat has been tampered with, i.e., baseball bat honed down to softball size.* RULING — *Dead ball and B1 is called out. Remove illegal piece of equipment from the game. This is an illegal bat.*

Sec. 32. ILLEGALLY BATTED BALL. An illegally batted ball occurs when:
a. A batter's entire foot is completely out of the box on the ground when he hits a ball fair or foul.
b. Any part of the batter's foot is touching home plate when he hits the ball.
c. The batter hits the ball with an illegal bat.

PLAY (1) — *Batter hits a pitched ball while his entire foot is completely out of batter's box, in contact with the ground, and the ball goes directly into the stand behind home plate.* RULING — *Ball is dead. Batter is declared out.*

PLAY (2) — *F1 delivers ball to B1. B1 has one foot touching home plate as he swings and misses pitch completely.* RULING — *A strike is called. This is not an illegally batted ball. The ball must be hit (fair or foul) to enforce the illegally batted ball rule.*

Sec. 33. ILLEGALLY CAUGHT BALL. An illegally caught ball occurs when a fielder catches a batted or thrown ball with his cap, mask, glove or any part of his uniform that is detached from its proper place.

PLAY — *REFER TO RULE 1, SECTION 12.*

▶**Sec. 34. ILLEGAL PLAYER.** A player who has entered the game without reporting. The use of an illegal player is removal of that player from the game, and once removed, he becomes an ineligible player.

▶**Sec. 35. INELIGIBLE PLAYER.** A player who can no longer legally participate in the game. The use of an ineligible player will constitute a forfeit.

Sec. 36. IN FLIGHT. In flight describes any batted, thrown or pitched ball which has not yet touched the ground or some object other than a fielder.

Sec. 37. IN JEOPARDY. In jeopardy is a term indicating that the ball is in play and an offensive player may be put out.

Sec. 38. INFIELD. The infield is that portion of the field in fair territory which includes areas normally covered by infielders.

Sec. 39. INFIELD FLY. An infield fly is a fair fly ball (not including a line drive or an attempted bunt) which can be caught by an infielder with ordinary effort when first and second or first, second and third bases are occupied, before two are out. The pitcher, catcher and any outfielder who positions himself in the infield on the play shall be considered infielders for the purposes of this rule.

NOTE: When it seems apparent that a batted ball will be an infield fly, the umpire shall immediately declare "INFIELD FLY - THE BATTER IS OUT" for the benefit of the runners. If the ball is near the foul lines, the umpire shall declare "INFIELD FLY - THE BATTER IS OUT IF FAIR."

The ball is alive and runners may advance at the risk of the ball being caught or retouched and advance after the ball is touched, the same as on any fly ball. If the hit becomes a foul ball, it is treated the same as any foul.

If a declared infield fly is allowed to fall untouched to the ground and bounces foul before passing first or third base, it is a foul ball. If a declared infield fly falls untouched to the ground outside the foul lines and bounces fair before passing first or third base, it is an infield fly.

PLAY (1) — *R1 and R2 are on second and first bases respectively, with none out. B3 hits a high pop foul between home and first base which F3 loses sight of in the sun. Ball lands on foul ground without being touched and rolls into fair territory halfway between home and first base. F1 picks up ball and throws to F4, covering first, who touches R2 with ball while runner R2 is off base.* RULING — *Infield fly. B3 and R2 are both out.*

PLAY (2) — *R1 and R2 are on second and first bases respectively, with one out. B3 hits a high fly ball which, in the judgement of the umpire, can be handled by the second baseman with reasonable effort. The "infield fly" rule is declared by the umpire. The second baseman intentionally drops the fly ball. R1, seeing the ball dropped, runs to third base but is thrown out.* RULING — *B3 is out on the "infield fly." The ball remains alive. R1 is also out since the infield fly takes precedence over the "intentionally dropped fly ball."*

Sec. 40. INNING. An inning is that portion of a game within which the teams alternate on offense and defense and in which there are three outs for each team. A new inning begins immediately after the final out of the previous inning.

Sec. 41. INTERFERENCE. Interference is the act of an offensive player or team member which impedes or confuses a defensive player attempting to execute a play.

Sec. 42. LEGAL TOUCH. A legal touch occurs when a runner or batter-baserunner who is not touching a base is touched by the ball while the ball is securely held in a fielder's hand. The ball is not considered as having been securely held if it is juggled or dropped by the fielder after having touched the runner, unless the runner deliberately knocks the ball from the hand of the fielder. It is sufficient for the runner to be touched with the hand or glove which holds the ball.

PLAY (1) — *B1 hits ground ball to first baseman who gathers in the ball, runs over to the first baseline, tags the runner, then juggles, bobbles and drops the ball.* RULING — *Illegal touch. Runner is safe.*

PLAY (2) — *The catcher has the ball in his glove when he tags runner with the glove. Ball does not come in contact with the runner.* RULING — *Touching with the glove or hand which holds the ball is the same as touching with the ball; the runner is out.*

PLAY (3) — *First baseman, while lying on the ground with ball in right hand tags first base with left hand prior to batter-baserunner reaching first base. RULING* — *Batter-baserunner is out. Legal touch.*

Sec. 43. LEGALLY CAUGHT BALL. A legally caught ball occurs when a fielder catches a batted or thrown ball, provided it is not caught in the fielder's hat, cap, mask, protector, pocket or other part of his uniform. It must be caught and firmly held with a hand or hands.

Sec. 44. LINE DRIVE. A line drive is a fly ball that is batted sharply and directly into the playing field.

Sec. 45. OBSTRUCTION. Obstruction is the act of:

a. A defensive player or team member which hinders or prevents a batter from striking or hitting a pitched ball.
b. A fielder, while not in possession of the ball, in the act of fielding a batted ball, or about to receive a thrown ball, which impedes the progress of a baserunner who is legally running bases.

Sec. 46. OFFENSIVE TEAM. The offensive team is the team at bat.

Sec. 47. OUTFIELD. The outfield is that portion of the field which is outside the diamond formed by the baselines or the area not normally covered by an infielder and within the foul lines beyond first and third bases and boundaries of the grounds.

Sec. 48. OVERSLIDE. An overslide is the act of an offensive player when, as a baserunner, he overslides a base he is attempting to reach. It is usually caused when his momentum causes him to lose contact with the base which then causes him to be in jeopardy. The batter-baserunner may overslide first base without being in jeopardy if he immediately returns to that base.

PLAY — *Baserunner overslides first base (a) during advance from home plate, or (b) on return to first base after attempt to advance to second base. In either case, he is tagged with ball while off base. RULING* — *(a) Safe, (b) Out.*

▶Sec. 49. **OVERTHROW.** An overthrow is a play in which a ball is thrown from one fielder to another to retire a runner and which goes into foul territory or goes beyond the boundary lines of the playing field (dead ball territory). Should the overthrow be ruled a blocked ball (Rule 1, Section 10) the ball is dead.

Sec. 50. PASSED BALL. (FP ONLY) A passed ball is a legally delivered ball that should have been held or controlled by the catcher with ordinary effort.

▶Sec. 51. **PIVOT FOOT.** (FP ONLY) The pivot foot is that foot which must remain in contact with the pitcher's plate. Pushing off with the pivot foot from a place other than the pitcher's plate is illegal.
(SP ONLY) The pivot foot is that foot which the pitcher must keep in constant contact with the pitcher's plate until the ball is released.

Sec. 52. PLAY BALL. "Play ball" is the term used by the plate umpire to indicate that the play shall begin or be resumed when the pitcher has the ball in his possession and is within eight feet (2.44 m) of the pitcher's plate. All defensive players, except the catcher who must be in his box, must be anywhere in fair ground to put the ball in play.

NOTE: (FP ONLY) See Rule 6, Section 7 for penalty.

Sec. 53. QUICK RETURN PITCH. A quick return pitch is one made by the pitcher with the obvious attempt to catch the batter off balance. This would be before the batter takes his desired position in the batter's box or while he is still off balance as a result of the previous pitch.

Sec. 54. RUNNER. The term "runner" means "batter-runner or baserunner."

Sec. 55. SACRIFICE FLY. A sacrifice fly is scored when, with less than two outs, the batter scores a runner with a fly ball which is caught.

Sec. 56. STARTING PITCHER. The player listed as a pitcher on the lineup card or official scorebook.

▶Sec. 57. **STEALING.** (FP ONLY). Stealing is the act of a baserunner attempting to advance during a pitch to the batter.

Sec. 58. STRIKE ZONE. (FP ONLY) The strike zone is that space over any part of home plate between the batter's arm pits and the top of his knees when the batter assumes a natural batting stance.
(SP ONLY) The strike zone is that space over any part of home plate between the batter's highest shoulder and his knees when the batter assumes a natural batting stance.

Sec. 59. TIME. "Time" is the term used by the umpire to order the suspension of play.

Sec. 60. TRIPLE PLAY. A triple play is a continuous action play by the defense in which three offensive players are put out.

Sec. 61. TURN AT BAT. A turn at bat begins when a player first enters the batter's box and continues until he is put out or becomes a baserunner.

Sec. 62. WILD PITCH. (FP ONLY) A wild pitch is a legally delivered ball so high, so low, or so wide of the plate that the catcher cannot, or does not, stop and control it with ordinary effort.

RULE 2. THE PLAYING FIELD

(Refer to Drawing Showing Official Dimensions of Softball Diamond)

Sec. 1. THE PLAYING FIELD IS THE AREA WITHIN WHICH THE BALL MAY BE LEGALLY PLAYED AND FIELDED. The playing field shall have a clear and unobstructed area within the radius of the prescribed fence distances from home plate between the foul lines. (Refer to FENCE DISTANCE Chart)

ADULT DIVISIONS	DISTANCES
Fast Pitch	
Female	200 ft. (60.96m)
Male	225 ft. (68.58m)
Modified	
Female	200 ft. (60.96m)
Male	265 ft. (80.80m)
Slow Pitch	
Female	250 ft. (76.20m)
Male	275 ft. (83.82m)
Co-Ed	275 ft. (83.82m)
Super	300 ft. (91.44m)
16" Slow Pitch	
Female	200 ft. (60.96m)
Male	250 ft. (76.20m)

YOUTH DIVISIONS	DISTANCES MINIMUM	MAXIMUM
Fast Pitch		
Girls 12-Under	175 ft. (53.34m)	200 ft. (60.96m)
Boys 12-Under	175 ft. (53.34m)	200 ft. (60.96m)
Girls 15-Under	175 ft. (53.34m)	200 ft. (60.96m)
Boys 15-Under	175 ft. (53.34m)	200 ft. (60.96m)
Girls 18-Under	200 ft. (60.96m)	225 ft. (68.58m)
Boys 18-Under	200 ft. (60.96m)	225 ft. (68.58m)
Slow Pitch		
Girls 12-Under	175 ft. (53.34m)	200 ft. (60.96m)
Boys 12-Under	175 ft. (53.34m)	200 ft. (60.96m)
Girls 15-Under	*225 ft. (68.58m)*	*250 ft. (76.20m)*
Boys 15-Under	*250 ft. (76.20m)*	*275 ft. (83.82m)*
Girls 18-Under	225 ft. (68.58m)	250 ft. (76.20m)
Boys 18-Under	275 ft. (83.82m)	300 ft. (91.44m)

Sec. 2. GROUND OR SPECIAL RULES ESTABLISHING THE LIMITS OF THE PLAYING FIELD MAY BE AGREED UPON BY LEAGUES OR OPPOSING TEAMS WHENEVER BACKSTOPS, FENCES, STANDS, VEHICLES, SPECTATORS OR OTHER OBSTRUCTIONS ARE WITHIN THE PRESCRIBED AREA. Any obstruction on fair ground less than the prescribed fence distances from home plate (as outlined in Section 1 of this rule) should be clearly marked for the umpire's information.

Sec. 3. THE OFFICIAL DIAMOND SHALL HAVE BASE LINES AS FOLLOWS:

ADULT DIVISIONS	DISTANCES	YOUTH DIVISIONS	DISTANCES
Fast Pitch		Fast Pitch	
Female	60 ft. (18.29m)	Girls 12-Under	60 ft. (18.29m)
Male	60 ft. (18.29m)	Boys 12-Under	60 ft. (18.29m)
		Girls 15-Under	60 ft. (18.29m)
		Boys 15-Under	60 ft. (18.29m)
Modified		Girls 18-Under	60 ft. (18.29m)
Female	60 ft. (18.29m)	Boys 18-Under	60 ft. (18.29m)
Male	60 ft. (18.29m)		
Slow Pitch		Slow Pitch	
Female	65 ft. (19.81m)	Girls 10-Under	50 ft. (15.24m)
Male	65 ft. (19.81m)	Boys 10-Under	50 ft. (15.24m)
Co-ed	65 ft. (19.81m)	Girls 12-Under	60 ft. (18.29m)
Super	65 ft. (19.81m)	Boys 12-Under	60 ft. (18.29m)
		Girls 15-Under	*65 ft. (19.81m)*
		Boys 15-Under	60 ft. (18.29m)
16" Slow Pitch		Girls 18-Under	65 ft. (19.81m)
Female	55 ft. (16.76m)	Boys 18-Under	65 ft. (19.81m)
Male	55 ft. (16.76m)		

THE OFFICIAL DIAMOND SHALL HAVE PITCHING DISTANCES AS FOLLOWS:

ADULT DIVISIONS	DISTANCES	YOUTH DIVISIONS	DISTANCES
Fast Pitch		Fast Pitch	
Female	40 ft. (12.19m)	Girls 12-Under	35 ft. (10.67m)
Male	46 ft. (14.02m)	Boys 12-Under	40 ft. (12.19m)
Modified		Girls 15-Under	40 ft. (12.19m)
Female	40 ft. (12.19m)	Boys 15-Under	46 ft. (14.02m)
Male	46 ft. (14.02m)	Girls 18-Under	40 ft. (12.19m)
Slow Pitch		Boys 18-Under	46 ft. (14.02m)
Female	46 ft. (14.02m)	Slow Pitch	
Male	46 ft. (14.02m)	Girls 10-Under	35 ft. (10.67m)
Co-ed	46 ft. (14.02m)	*Boys 10-Under*	*35 ft. (10.67m)*
Super	46 ft. (14.02m)	Girls 12-Under	40 ft. (12.19m)
16" Slow Pitch		Boys 12-Under	40 ft. (12.19m)
Female	38 ft. (11.58m)	*Girls 15-Under*	*46 ft. (14.02m)*
Male	38 ft. (11.58m)	Boys 15-Under	46 ft. (14.02m)
		Girls 18-Under	46 ft. (14.02m)
		Boys 18-Under	46 ft. (14.02m)

Sec. 4. FOR THE LAYOUT OF THE DIAMOND, REFER TO DRAWING SHOWING OFFICIAL DIMENSIONS OF SOFTBALL DIAMOND. THIS SECTION IS AN EXAMPLE FOR LAYING OUT A DIAMOND WITH 60 FOOT BASES AND A 46 FOOT PITCHING DISTANCE. To determine the position of home plate, draw a line in the direction it is desired to lay the diamond. Drive a stake at the corner of home plate nearest the catcher. Fasten a cord to this stake and tie knots or otherwise mark the cord at 46 feet (14.02m), 60 feet (18.29m), 84 feet 10¼ inches (25.86m) and at 120 feet (36.58m).

Place the cord (without stretching) along the direction line and place a stake at the 46 foot (14.02m) marker — this will be the front line at the middle of the pitcher's plate. Along the same line, drive a stake at the 84 foot 10¼ inch (25.68m) marker. This will be the center of second base. For the 65 foot base distance, this line will be 91 feet 11 inches (28.07m).

Place the 120 foot (36.58m) marker at the center of second base and, taking hold of the cord at the 60 foot (18.29m) marker, walk to the right of the direction line until the cord is taut and drive a stake at the 60 foot (18.29m) marker. This will be the outside corner of first base and the cord will now form the lines to first and second bases. Again, holding the cord at the 60 foot (18.29m) marker, walk across the field and in like manner, mark the outside corner of third base. Home plate, first and third bases are wholly inside the diamond.

To check the diamond, place the home plate end of the cord at the first base stake and the 120 foot (36.58m) marker at third base. The 60 foot (18.29m) marker should now check at home plate and second base.

In laying out a 65 foot base path diamond, follow the same procedure with the following substitute dimensions: 65 feet (19.81m), 130 foot (39.62m), and 91 feet, 11 inches (28.07m). Check all distances with a steel tape whenever possible.

a. **THE THREE FOOT (0.91m) LINE** is drawn parallel to and three feet (0.91m) from the baseline starting at a point halfway between home plate and first base.
b. **THE BATTER'S ON-DECK CIRCLE** is a five foot (1.52m) circle [2½ foot (0.76m) radius] placed adjacent to the end of player's bench or dugout area closest to home plate.
c. **THE BATTER'S BOX,** one on each side of home plate, shall measure three feet (0.91m) wide by seven feet (2.13m). The inside lines of the batter's box shall be six inches (15.24cm) from home plate. The front line of the box shall be four feet (1.22m) in front of a line drawn through the center of home plate. The lines are considered as being within the batter's box.
d. **THE CATCHER'S BOX** shall be 10 feet (3.05m) in length from the rear outside corners of the batter's boxes and shall be eight feet two inches (2.57m) wide.
e. **THE COACH'S BOX IS BEHIND A LINE 15 FEET (4.57m) LONG DRAWN OUTSIDE THE DIAMOND.** The line is parallel to and eight feet (2.44m) from the first and third baselines, extended from the bases toward home plate.
f. **THE PITCHER'S PLATE** shall be permanently attached to the ground at distances indicated in Rule 2, Sec. 3. (FP Only) There shall be a 16 foot (4.88m) circle drawn from the pitcher's plate, eight feet (2.44m) in radius. The lines drawn around the pitcher's plate are considered inside the circle.

RULE 3. EQUIPMENT

Sec. 1. THE OFFICIAL BAT.

a. Shall be made of one piece of hardwood, or formed from a block of wood consisting of two or more pieces of wood bonded together with an adhesive in such a way that the grain direction of all pieces is essentially parallel to the length of the bat.
b. Shall be plastic, bamboo, graphite, metal, magnesium or any combination of these materials.
c. Can be laminated, but must contain only wood or adhesive and have a clear finish (if finished).
d. Shall be round or three sided, and shall be smooth. If the barrel end has knurled finish, the maximum surface roughness is no more than 250 if measured by a profilometer, or 4/1000 if measured by a spectrograph.
e. Shall not be more than 34 inches (87.0 cm) long, nor exceed 38 ounces (1100.0 g) in weight.
f. If round, shall not be more than 2¼ inches (6.0 cm) in diameter at its largest part; and if three sided, shall not exceed 2¼ inches (6.0 cm) on the hitting surface. A tolerance of 1/32 inches (0.80 mm) is permitted to allow for expansion on the round bat.
g. If metal, may be angular.
h. Shall not have exposed rivets, pins, rough or sharp edges, or any form of exterior fastener that would present a hazard. A metal bat shall be free of burrs.
i. If metal, shall not have a wooden handle.
j. Shall have a safety grip of cork, tape (not smooth plastic type) or composition material. The safety grip shall not be less than 10 inches (25.0 cm) or shall not extend more than 15 inches (40.0 cm) from the small end of the bat. A molded finger-formed grip made by the manufacturer, if used, must be permanently attached to the bat. Resin, pine tar, or spray substances placed on the safety grip to enhance the grip, is permissible on the grip only. NOTE: Tape applied to any bat must be continuously spiral. It does not have to be a solid layer of tape. It cannot exceed two layers.
k. If metal, and not made of one piece construction with the barrel end closed, shall have a rubber or vinyl plastic insert firmly secured at the large end of the bat.
l. Shall have a safety knob of a minimum of one-fourth inch protruding at a 90-degree angle from the handle. It can be molded, lathed, welded or permanently fastened. A "flare or cone" grip attached to the bat will be considered an altered bat.
m. Shall be marked "OFFICIAL SOFTBALL" by the manufacturer. If the words, "OFFICIAL SOFTBALL" cannot be read due to wear and tear on the bat, the bat should be declared legal if it is legal in all other aspects.

Beginning in 1987, softball bats used in A.S.A. championship tournament play must be approved by the Equipment Standards Committee.

NOTE: Bats with special design features to enhance hit distance will not be allowed.

Sec. 2. WARM-UP BATS. No more than two official softball bats, one A.S.A. approved warm-up bat, or a combination of the two — not to exceed two — may be used by the on-deck batter in the on-deck circle. The WARM-UP BAT should meet the following requirements to be approved: a) stamped with one-fourth inch letters WB on either end of the bat; b) a minimum weight of 48 ounces (1360.0 g); c) a minimum barrel diameter of 2½ inches (6.0 cm); d) have a safety grip of at least 10 inches (25.0 cm) and no more than 15 inches (40.0 cm) extended from the knob; and/or e) be of one piece construction or a one-piece permanently assembled bat approved by the Equipment Standards Committee.

Sec. 3. THE OFFICIAL SOFTBALL.

a. Shall be a regular, smooth-seamed, concealed stitched or flat surfaced ball.
b. Shall have a center core made of either No. 1 quality, long fibre kapok, a mixture of cork and rubber, a polyurethane mixture or other materials approved by the A.S.A.
c. May be hand or machine wound, with a fine quality twisted yarn, and covered with latex or rubber cement.
d. Shall have a cover cemented to the ball by application of cement to the underside of the cover, and sewn with waxed thread of cotton or linen, or shall have a molded cover bonded to the core with an authentic fascimile of stitching as approved by the ASA.
e. Shall have a cover of chrome tanned top grain horsehide or cowhide; synthetic material; or made of other materials approved by the A.S.A.
f. The 12-inch (30.0 cm) ball shall be between 11-7/8 inches (30.0 cm) and 12-1/8 inches (31.0 cm) in circumference, and shall weigh between 6¼ ounces (180.0 g) and 7 ounces (200.0 g). The smooth-seam style shall not have less than 88 stitches in each cover, sewn by the two-needle method, or with an authentic fascimile of stitching as approved by the ASA.
g. The 11-inch (27.0 cm) ball shall be between 10-7/8 inches (27.0 cm) and 11-1/8 inches (28.0 cm) in circumference, and shall weigh between 5-7/8 ounces (165.0 g) and 6-1/8 ounces (175.0 g). The smooth-seam style shall not have less than 80 stitches in each cover, sewn by the two-needle method, or with an authentic fascimile of stitching as approved by the ASA.
▶ h. The white-stitch 12 inch ball shall be used in the following ASA championship play: Men's and Women's fast pitch, Boys' Junior Olympic Fast Pitch and Slow Pitch and Girls' Junior Olympic Fast Pitch. Beginning in 1989 it must have a COR of .50 or under and be so marked.
i. The red-stitch 12 inch ball with a COR of .47 and under shall be used in all adult men's slow pitch and Co-Ed slow pitch, and must have a marking of MSP-47.
j. The red-stitch 11 inch ball with a COR of .47 and under shall be used in the following ASA Play: Women's Slow Pitch and all Girls' Junior Olympic Slow Pitch. It must have a GWSP-47 marking.
k. Softballs used in A.S.A. championship tournament play must meet standards set by the A.S.A. Equipment Standards Committee as shown below, and must be stamped with the ASA logo.

THE OFFICIAL SOFTBALL SPECIFICATIONS ARE AS FOLLOWS:

SOFTBALL	THREAD COLOR	MINIMUM SIZE	MAXIMUM SIZE	MINIMUM SIZE	MAXIMUM SIZE	MARKING
12-inch FP (30.0 cm)	white	11 7/8 in 30.0 cm	12 1/8 in 31.0 cm	6¼ oz 180.0 g	7 oz 200.0 g	A.S.A. LOGO
12-inch SP (30.0 cm)	red	11 7/8 in 30.0 cm	12 1/8 in 31.0 cm	6¼ oz 180.0 g	7 oz 200.0 g	MSP-47
16-inch SP (41.0 cm)	white	15 7/8 in 40.0 cm	16 1/8 in 41.0 cm	9 oz 225.0 g	10 oz 283.0 g	
11-inch (27.0 cm)	red	10 7/8 in 27.0 cm	11 1/8 in 28.0 cm	5 7/8 oz 165.0 g	6 1/8 oz 175.0 g	GWSP-47

Sec. 4. THE HOME PLATE SHALL BE MADE OF RUBBER OR OTHER SUITABLE MATERIALS. It shall be a five-sided figure, 17 inches (43.18cm) wide across the edge facing the pitcher. The sides shall be parallel to the inside lines of the batter's box and shall be eight and one-half inches (21.59cm) long. The sides of the point facing the catcher shall be 12 inches (30.48cm) long.

Sec. 5. THE PITCHER'S PLATE shall be of wood or rubber, 24 inches (60.96cm) long and six inches (15.24cm) wide. The top of the plate shall be level with the ground. The front line of the plate shall be the prescribed pitching distances from the outside corner of home plate. (Refer to PITCHING DISTANCES Chart in Rule 2, Section 3.)

Sec. 6. THE BASES. OTHER THAN HOME PLATE, SHALL BE 15 INCHES (38.10cm) SQUARE, MADE OF CANVAS OR OTHER SUITABLE MATERIALS, AND NOT MORE THAN FIVE INCHES (12.70cm) IN THICKNESS. The bases should be securely fastened in position.

a. *The double base is approved for use at first base. This base is 15 by 30 inches, made of canvas or other suitable material. Half the base is white (secured in fair territory) and half is orange (secured in foul territory). It should not be more than five inches (12.70cm) in thickness.*

NOTE: *The following rules apply to the double base:*

1) A batted ball hitting the white portion is declared fair, and a batted ball hitting the orange portion is declared foul.
2) Both white and orange portions of the base are treated equally for the offense and the defense.
REFER TO POINTS OF EMPHASIS

SOFTBALL GLOVE SPECIFICATIONS

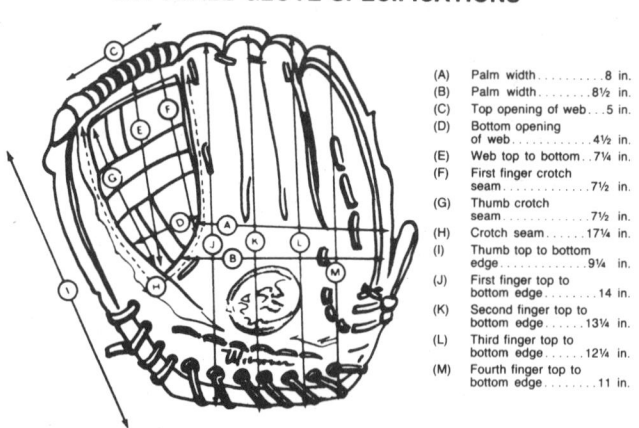

(A) Palm width.........8 in.
(B) Palm width.........8½ in.
(C) Top opening of web...5 in.
(D) Bottom opening of web...........4½ in.
(E) Web top to bottom..7¼ in.
(F) First finger crotch seam..............7½ in.
(G) Thumb crotch seam..............7½ in.
(H) Crotch seam......17¼ in.
(I) Thumb top to bottom edge..............9¼ in.
(J) First finger top to bottom edge........14 in.
(K) Second finger top to bottom edge......13¼ in.
(L) Third finger top to bottom edge......12¼ in.
(M) Fourth finger top to bottom edge........11 in.

Sec. 7. GLOVES MAY BE WORN BY ANY PLAYER, BUT MITTS MAY BE USED ONLY BY THE CATCHER AND FIRST BASEMAN. No top lacing, webbing or other device between the thumb and body of the glove or mitt worn by a first baseman or other fielder shall be more than five inches (12.70cm) in length. The pitcher's glove shall be of one solid color, other than white or grey. Multicolored gloves are acceptable for all other players. Gloves with white or grey circles on the outside, giving the appearance of a ball, are illegal for all players.

Sec. 8. SHOES MUST BE WORN BY ALL PLAYERS. A SHOE SHALL BE CON-

SIDERED OFFICIAL IF IT IS MADE WITH EITHER CANVAS OR LEATHER UPPERS OR SIMILAR MATERIALS. The soles may be either smooth or have soft or hard rubber cleats. Ordinary metal sole and heel plates may be used if the spikes on the plates do not extend more than three-fourths of an inch (1.91cm) from the sole or heel of the shoe. Shoes with rounded metal spikes are illegal.

YOUTH/CO-ED PLAY: No metal spikes are allowed in any division of youth or co-ed play. No hard plastic or polyurethane spikes similar to metal sole and heel plate are allowed in any division of youth or co-ed play. No shoes with detachable cleats that screw ON are allowed; however shoes with detachable cleats that screw INTO the shoe are allowed.

> *PLAY — Players from Team B are wearing (a) golf shoes, (b) track shoes, (c) metal baseball spikes, (d) coaches shoes with ripple rubber soles. RULING — (a) and (b) Illegal; (c) and (d) Legal.*

Sec. 9. MASKS, BODY PROTECTORS, AND SHIN GUARDS.
a. (FP ONLY) Masks, with throat protectors, must be worn by adult catchers, and youth catchers must wear mask, throat protector and helmet. (SP ONLY) Youth catchers must wear mask with helmet and it is recommended in adult slow pitch. An extended wire protector can be worn in lieu of throat protector attached to the mask.
b. Body protectors are recommended for catchers in fast pitch. Youth catchers must wear body protectors in fast pitch and it is recommended they wear body protectors in slow pitch.
c. Youth fast pitch catchers must wear shin guards, and it is recommended for adult fast pitch.

> *PLAY (1) — Adult catcher refuses to wear a mask in (a) slow pitch, (b) fast pitch. RULING — (a) Legal, (b) Illegal. Catcher must wear a mask in fast pitch and all youth catchers must wear masks with helmets.*

> *PLAY (2) — (FP ONLY) Catcher refuses to wear his mask after being ordered to wear a mask by the umpire. RULING — Forfeited game shall be declared by the umpire if no one else will wear mask and catch.*

Sec. 10. NO EQUIPMENT SHALL BE LEFT LYING ON THE FIELD, EITHER IN FAIR OR FOUL TERRITORY. (See Rule 8, Section 5g-Play 4) All non-player equipment — including wheelchairs, crutches and other similar items — shall be confined to out-of-play areas.

▶**Sec. 11. UNIFORM.** All players on a team shall wear uniforms alike in color, trim and style. Pants should be either all long or all short in style. Coaches must be neatly attired, dressed alike, or in team uniform and in accordance with the color code of the team.
a. Ball caps must be alike and are:
  1. Mandatory for all male players and must be worn properly.
  2. Optional for female players. Visors and headbands are also optional for female players, but may not be mixed. All female players are not required to wear headwear, but those players with headware must be alike. Handkerchiefs do not qualify as headbands and cannot be worn, either around the head or around the neck.
b. Players may wear a uniform, solid colored undershirt (it may be white). It is not mandatory that all players wear an undershirt if one player wears one, but those that are worn must be alike. No player may wear ragged, frayed, or slit sleeves on exposed undershirts.
c. An **arabic** number of contrasting color, at least six inches (15.24cm) high, must be worn on the back of all uniform shirts. No players on the same team may wear identical numbers. (Number 3 and 03 are examples of identical numbers.) Players without numbers will not be permitted to play. If duplicate numbers exist, one will not be permitted to play in the game.
d. Helmets are permissible for adult batters, pitchers, baserunners and catchers. Other than catchers and pitchers, helmets may not be worn by any other defensive player in adult and youth play, except for medical purposes. (JO Fast and Slow Pitch) Helmets with ear flaps are mandatory for all Junior Olympic batters and baserunners. (Players not wearing helmets will not be allowed to participate.) The helmets must be NOC-SAE and ASA approved. Effective 1987.

> NOTE: Catcher helmets at the present time do not have NOCSAE standards and no stamp will be required on this helmet.

e. Casts (plaster or other hard substance in its final form) may not be worn during the game. Any exposed metal may be considered legal if covered by soft material and taped.
▶f. Exposed jewelry such as wrist watches, bracelets, large or loop type earrings and neck chains, or any other item judged dangerous by the umpire, may not be worn during the game. Medical alert bracelets or necklaces are not considered jewelry, but if worn, they must be taped to the body.

> *PLAY (1) — A female team has three players wearing caps and the remaining players do not wear anything on their heads. RULING — Legal, if the three hats are alike. All female players do not have to wear hats, nor can they mix headbands and hats.*

> *PLAY (2) — Two female players wear caps and the remaining players wear similar colored headbands. RULING — Illegal. Either caps or headbands may be worn, but not both.*

> *PLAY (3) — In Co-Ed play, four males wear caps, one does not, two females have headbands, and three do not. RULING—Illegal. It is okay for female players not to wear headbands or caps, but all male players must wear caps. The rest of the uniform should be similar (ie. all players in shorts or all in long pants, the same jerseys and leggings, etc.)*

> *PLAY (4) — Player F1 wears (a) uniform number 6 on the back of his jersey, (b) uniform number 00 on the back of his jersey, (c) no uniform number on the jersey, but number 5 on the pants, (d) uniform number on the back of the jersey, but a two inch number on the front, (e) no uniform number at all. RULING—Legal in (a) and (b), not legal in (c), (d), or (e).*

> *PLAY (5) — Player F1 (Jones) was listed in the scorebook with the wrong number and (a) had his name on the jersey, (b) no name on the jersey. RULING: Correct the number in the scorebook in either case and resume play. There is no penalty.*

RULE 4. PLAYERS & SUBSTITUTES

Sec. 1. A TEAM SHALL CONSIST OF:
a. Fast Pitch - 9 Players.
b. Fast Pitch with a Designated Player - 10 Players.
c. Slow Pitch - 10 Players.
d. Slow Pitch with an Extra Player - 11 Players.
e. Male rosters shall include only male players and female rosters shall include only female players.
f. Co-Ed - 10 Players (five male and five female).
g. *Co-Ed Slow Pitch with Extra Players — 12 players (six male and six female). NOTE: If the EP is used in Co-Ed, 12 players must be used. It is not permissible to use 11 players because of the alternate batters.*

Sec. 2. PLAYERS' POSITIONS SHALL BE DESIGNATED AS FOLLOWS:
a. Fast Pitch: Pitcher, catcher, first baseman, second baseman, third baseman, shortstop, left fielder, center fielder and right fielder.
b. Fast Pitch with a Designated Hitter: Same as Fast Pitch in paragraph "a" above, plus a "designated hitter."
c. Slow Pitch: Same as Fast Pitch in paragraph "a" above, plus a "short fielder."

> NOTE: Players of the team in the field may be stationed anywhere on fair territory, except the catcher, who must be in the catcher's box, and the pitcher, who must be in a legal pitching position at the start of each pitch. (FP Only) When a pitch is delivered without all defensive players in fair territory, an illegal pitch shall be declared.

d. Co-Ed defensive positioning shall include two males and two females in the outfield, two males and two females in the infield, and one male and one female in the pitcher-catcher positions. Once determining positions, the players must be stationed in fair ground, except the catcher as indicated in the "note" above.

Sec. 3. DESIGNATED PLAYER (FP ONLY)
a. *A designated player, referred to as a "DP" may be used for any player, provided it is made known prior to the start of the game and his name is indicated on the line-up sheet or score sheet. Failure to complete the game with a "DP" results in forfeiture of the game.*
b. *The player listed as "DP" must remain in the same position in the batting order for the entire game. The starting player and his substitute(s) cannot be in the game at the same time. The starting "DP" may re-enter one time.*
c. *The "DP" may be substituted for at any time, either by a pinch-hitter, pinch-runner, or by the defensive player being hit for. If the substitute is the defensive player, he must bat in the same order as the "DP" and use of the "DP" will then be terminated. If the substitute is a pinch-runner or pinch-hitter, it must be a player who has not yet been in the game, and that substitute then becomes the "DP" for the remainder of the game, or until substituted for, or until the starting "DP" re-enters the game.*
d. *The "DP" may play defense in any position. Should the "DP" play defense for a player other than the player he is batting for, that player will continue to bat, but not play defense.*

▶NOTE: The player's name who the "DP" is batting for will be placed in the tenth position in the scorebook.

> *PLAY (1) — In the fifth inning, Jones comes into the game as a DP and is placed at the end of the batting order. RULING — Illegal. The DP must be announced prior to the start of the game and his name entered on the starting lineup. If one pitch is thrown to Jones, he is considered an illegal substitute for the player listed number one on the batting order.*

> *PLAY (2) — At the beginning of the game, Jones is put in the lineup as a DP for Smith. In the third inning Smith is injured and has to leave the game. Jones replaces Smith as shortstop. RULING — Legal.*

> *PLAY (3) — Jones begins the game at second base, but does not bat. In the fourth inning he takes the place of Smith as the DP. RULING — Legal. The role of the DP is terminated for the remainder of the game.*

Sec. 4. EXTRA PLAYER (SP ONLY)
a. *An extra player, referred to as an "EP" is optional, but if one is used, it must be made known prior to the start of the game, and be listed on the scoring sheet in the regular batting order. If the "EP" is used, he must be used the entire game. Failure to complete the game with the "EP" results in forfeiture of the game.*
b. *The "EP" must remain in the same position in the batting order for the entire game.*
c. *If an "EP" is used, all eleven must bat and any ten can play defense. Defensive positions can be changed, but the batting order must remain the same.*
d. *The "EP" may be substituted for at any time, either by a pinch-runner or pinch-hitter, who then becomes the "EP." The substitute must be a player who has not yet been in the game. The starting "EP" can re-enter.*
e. *The "EP" is used in Co-Ed, all twelve (12) must bat and any ten (10) — five male and five female — can play defense. Defensive positions can be changed as long as the following ratio is used: two male/two female in the outfield, two male/two female in the infield and one male/one female as pitcher/catcher. The batting order must remain the same throughout the game.*

Sec. 5. RE-ENTRY
Any of the starting players, including a "DP" (FP ONLY) or an "EP" (SP ONLY), may be withdrawn and re-entered once, provided players occupy the same batting positions whenever in the lineup.
EXCEPTION: When the defensive player bats for the "DP" (FP ONLY), the "DP" is eliminated and may not re-enter.

NOTE: The original player and the substitute(s) cannot be in the lineup at the same time.

a. Violation of the re-entry rule results in the use of an illegal player. *An ejection of both the manager and the illegal player shall be declared when the violation is brought to the attention of the umpire by the offended team.*
b. Violation of the re-entry rule is handled as a protest, which can be made anytime DURING THE GAME. The protest need not be made prior to the next pitch, as described in Rule 11, Section 7c.

PLAY — In the top half of the first inning with two outs, R1 on first base, B4 (Smith) is announced on the PA system. Just then the manager decides to substitute Jones. Jones strikes out. In the third inning, Smith, who was announced in the first inning, pinch-hits for Jones. *RULING* — Legal. Members of the starting lineup may be withdrawn and re-entered one time, provided they occupy the same batting positions they held when originally in the lineup.

Sec. 6. A TEAM MUST HAVE THE REQUIRED NUMBER OF PLAYERS PRESENT TO START OR CONTINUE A GAME. Requirements are:
a. Fast Pitch - 9 Players.
b. Fast Pitch with a Designated Player - 10 Players. If terminated as allowed in section 3c, the game can continue with 9 players.
c. Slow Pitch - 10 Players.
d. Slow Pitch with an Extra Player - 11 Players.
e. Co-ed Slow Pitch — 10 Players (five male and five female)
f. Co-Ed Slow Pitch with two Extra Players — 12 players (six male and six female)

PENALTY: Game is forfeited. [See Rule 5, Section 3f(7)]

NOTE: Players listed on the starting lineup and not available at game time may be substituted for and re-entered under the Re-Entry Rule.

Sec. 7. A PLAYER SHALL BE OFFICIALLY IN THE GAME WHEN HIS NAME HAS BEEN ENTERED ON THE OFFICIAL SCORESHEET OR HAS BEEN ANNOUNCED. A substitute may take the place of a player whose name is in his team's batting order. The following regulations govern the substitution of players:

a. The manager or team representative of the team making the substitution shall immediately notify the plate umpire at the time a substitute enters, who shall report the change to the scorer prior to the next pitch. If the violation is discovered prior to a pitch being made (legal or illegal), there is no penalty and the illegal substitute shall be declared legal.

▶ The illegal substitute is considered in the game if a pitch has been made (legal or illegal). OFFENSE: (1) If the illegal player is discovered while at bat, he is declared an illegal player and a legal substitute assumes the ball and strike count. Any advance of baserunners while the illegal batter is at bat, is legal. (2) If the illegal player is discovered after completing his turn at bat and prior to the next pitch, the illegal player is called out, ruled ineligible, and any advance of baserunners as a result of a walk or base hit by the illegal batter, is nullified. (3) If the illegal player is discovered after completing his turn at bat and after the next pitch, the illegal player is ruled ineligible and any advance by baserunners while the illegal batter was at bat, is legal.

NOTE: When the illegal substitute is ruled ineligible, he is removed from the game. If he further participates after being discovered, the game is declared a forfeit (Rule 1, Section 35)

Violation of the illegal substitute is handled as a protest by the offended team. All other substitutes are considered in the game as described in Rule 4, Section 7b.

PLAY (1) — Jones, a legal substitute, enters the game in the third inning unreported. In the fifth inning, the opponents report this to the umpire, or the scorekeeper reports this to the umpire. RULING: The player (Jones) is immediately removed. All play by or on Jones is legal. A legal substitute must be reported into the game.

PLAY (2) — Smith re-enters the game unreported in the fourth inning for his substitute. After he hits the ball and reaches first base safely, it is detected by the opponent and reported to the umpire. RULING: Smith is called out, ruled ineligible and a legal substitute must enter the game. If a substitute is not available, the game if forfeited.

PLAY (3) — Brown replaces Carter, a starting player, in the third inning. Carter re-enters the game in the sixth inning for Green, another starting player. Carter singles and the opponents bring to the attention of the umpire that Carter's re-entry was not reported. RULING: This is a violation of the re-entry rule since Carter did not replace his substitute, thus the game shall be forfeited under Rule 4, Section 5a.

b. Substitute players will be considered in the game after one pitch has been thrown:
(1) If a batter, when he's in the batter's box.
(2) If a fielder, when he's in a defensive position.
(3) If a runner, when on the base he is holding.
(4) If a pitcher, when he's near pitcher's plate.
c. Any player may be removed from the game during any dead ball.

PLAY (1) — Jones is the starting pitcher. In the top of the third inning Smith bats for Jones. In the bottom of the third Jones returns to pitch. RULING: Legal.

PLAY (2) — Pitcher Jones walks B3 and is replaced by Smith. The offense substitutes B11 for B4 and before Smith throws one pitch (a) Jones, the starting pitcher, re-enters, (b) Brown is substituted for Smith. RULING: Legal in both situations. The pitcher no longer has to pitch until the first batter facing him has completed his turn at bat, the side has been retired or he has been removed from the game.

d. A player removed from the game shall not participate in the game again, except as a coach.
EXCEPTION: The starting lineup may re-enter one time. (See Rule 4, Section 5)
EFFECT - Sec. 7d: The game shall be forfeited to the offended team.

RULE 5. THE GAME

Sec. 1. THE CHOICE OF THE FIRST OR LAST BAT IN THE INNING SHALL BE DECIDED BY A TOSS OF A COIN, UNLESS OTHERWISE STATED IN THE RULES OF THE ORGANIZATION UNDER WHICH THE SCHEDULE OF GAMES IS BEING PLAYED.

Sec. 2. THE FITNESS OF THE GROUND FOR A GAME SHALL BE DECIDED SOLELY BY THE PLATE UMPIRE.

Sec. 3. A REGULATION GAME SHALL CONSIST OF SEVEN INNINGS.
a. A full seven innings need not be played if the team second at bat scores more runs in six innings or before the third out in the last of the seventh inning.
b. A game that is tied at the end of seven innings shall be continued by playing additional innings; or until one side has scored more runs than the other at the end of a complete inning; or until the team second at bat has scored more runs in their half of the inning before the third out is made.
c. A game called by the umpire shall be regulation if five or more complete innings have been played or if the team second at bat has scored more runs in four or more innings than the other team has scored in five or more innings. The umpire is empowered to call a game at any time because of darkness, rain, fire, panic or other causes which places the patrons or players in peril.

PLAY — At the end of the fourth inning, the score is H1 and V2. There is no score in the first half of the fifth, but in the last half H scores: (a) 1 run; (b) two runs. In either case, game is called for rain with only one or two outs. RULING — In either case, it is a regulation game. In (a), it is a tie game, but all records count. In (b), H is the winner.

d. A regulation tie game shall be declared if the score is equal when the game is called at the end of five or more complete innings or if the team second at bat has equaled the score of the first team at bat in the incomplete inning.

PLAY — In the last half of the sixth inning, with R1, R2 and R3 on third, second and first bases respectively, B4 hits a home run, tying the score 6 to 6. It then begins to rain heavily and, eventually, forces the umpire to call the game. RULING — The game ends in a 6 to 6 tie.

e. These provisions do not apply to any acts on the part of players or spectators which might call for forfeiture of the game. The umpire may forfeit the game if attacked physically by any team member or spectator.
f. A forfeited game shall be declared by the umpire in favor of the team not at fault in the following cases:
(1) If a team fails to appear on the field or, being on the field, refuses to begin a game for which it is scheduled or assigned at the time scheduled or within a time set for forfeitures by the organization in which the team is playing.
(2) If after the game has begun, one side refuses to continue to play, unless the game has been suspended or terminated by the umpire.

PLAY — A game is called after seven complete innings of play because the manager of the visiting team no longer wishes to play. RULING — If weather permits, the game shall not be terminated. The umpire shall forfeit the game to the home team by a score of 7-0.

(3) If, after play has been suspended by the umpire, one side fails to resume playing within two minutes after the umpire has called "play ball."
(4) If a team employs tactics noticeably designed to delay or to hasten the game.
(5) If, after warning by the umpire, any one of the rules of the game is willfully violated.
(6) If the order for the removal of a player is not obeyed within one minute.
(7) If, because of the removal of the players from the game by the umpire or for any cause, there are less than nine (Fast Pitch), 10 (Fast Pitch with DP), 10 (Slow Pitch), or 11 (Slow Pitch with EP), or 12 (Co-Ed Slow Pitch with two EP's) on either team.
EXCEPTION: If a team starts the game with a DP (FP ONLY) and the defensive player bats for the DP, (Rule 4, Section 3c) the team must continue and end the game with nine players.

PLAY — A team starts a game with 10 players in slow pitch or nine players in fast pitch, but loses one player due to injury and has no substitute to replace the injured player. RULING — The game is forfeited to the opponent. A team may not continue a game with less than the number of players required to start the game.

g. Games that are not considered regulation or regulation tie games shall be replayed from the beginning. Original lineups may be changed when the game is replayed.
EXCEPTION: A.S.A. PROCEDURAL CODE 9.01(a) states that during all championship tournament play, (district, metro, state, regional, or national tournament), in the event of rain or any cause which interrupts a game, the game must be resumed at the exact point where it was stopped.

Sec. 4. THE WINNER OF THE GAME SHALL BE THE TEAM THAT SCORES THE MOST RUNS IN A REGULATION GAME.
a. The score of a called regulation game shall be the score at the end of the last complete inning, unless the team second at bat has scored more runs than the first team at bat in the incomplete inning. In this case, the score shall be that of the incomplete inning.
b. The score of a regulation tie game shall be the tie score when the game was terminated. A regulation tie game shall be replayed from the beginning.
c. The score of a forfeited game shall be 7-0 in favor of the team not at fault.

Sec. 5. ONE RUN SHALL BE SCORED EACH TIME A BASERUNNER LEGALLY TOUCHES FIRST, SECOND, THIRD BASES AND HOME PLATE BEFORE THE THIRD OUT OF THE INNING.

Sec. 6. A RUN SHALL NOT BE SCORED IF THE THIRD OUT OF THE INNING IS A RESULT OF:
a. The batter being put out before legally touching first base.
b. A baserunner being forced out due to the batter becoming a baserunner.

PLAY (1) — R1 is on third base and R2 is on first base with two outs. Batter hits ground ball to F4, who chases R2 back toward first base and tags him (a) before R1 scores, (b) after R1 scores. RULING — Run does not count in (a) or (b) since the third out was a force-out.

PLAY (2) — With one out and runners on second base and third base, the batter flies out for the second out. The runner on third base tags up after the catch, but the runner on second base does not. The runner on third base crosses

66

the plate before an appeal is made at second base. RULING — The run will count, as this is a time play and not a force out. If the runner crosses home plate after the appeal, the run would not count.

c. (FP ONLY) A baserunner leaving base before the pitcher releases the ball to the batter. (SP ONLY) A baserunner leaving base before the pitched ball reaches home plate or before the pitched ball is batted.

Sec. 7. NO SUCCEEDING RUNNER SHALL SCORE A RUN WHEN A PRECEDING RUNNER HAS BEEN DECLARED THE THIRD OUT OF AN INNING.

PLAY (1) — One out, R1 on third base and R2 on second base. Batter hits a fly ball which is caught by F7. R1 tags up and leaves his base before the fly ball is touched by F7. R2 tags up and legally leaves his base and scores. Appeal is made at third base and umpire declares R1 out. RULING — Three outs, no runs score.

PLAY (2) — Two outs, R1 on third base, R2 on second base and R3 on first base. Batter hits ball over the fence for a home run. R1 fails to touch home plate but R2, R3 and the batter-baserunner touch all bases in regular order, including home plate. An appeal is made on R1 at home plate. Umpire declares R1 out. RULING — No runs score.

Sec. 8. A BASERUNNER SHALL NOT SCORE A RUN AHEAD OF THE BASERUNNER PRECEDING HIM IN THE BATTING ORDER, IF THE PRECEDING RUNNER HAS NOT BEEN PUT OUT.

Sec. 9. THERE SHALL BE ONLY ONE CHARGED CONFERENCE BETWEEN THE MANAGER OR OTHER TEAM REPRESENTATIVE AND THE BATTER OR BASERUNNER IN AN INNING. Umpires shall not permit any such conferences in excess of one in an inning.

PENALTY: Ejection of manager or coach who insists on another charged conference.

▶**Sec. 10. HOME RUN CLASSIFICATION (SP ONLY).** A limit of over-the-fence home runs will be used in all Men's and Co-Ed slow pitch divisions. All balls hit over the fence in a game by a team in excess of the following limits will be ruled a foul ball, and if a foul ball is a third strike, the batter is out.
　Super Classification — Unlimited
　Major Classification — Twelve (12)
　Class "A" Classification — Five (5)
　Class "B" Classification — Three (3)
　Class "C" Classification — One (1)
　Masters Classification — Three (3)
　Co-Ed Classification — Three (3)

NOTE: Any ball touched by a defensive player, which then goes over the fence in fair territory, shall not be included in the total of over-the-fence home runs.

PLAY (1) — Bases loaded with two outs. Class 'A' slow pitch tournament with a five (5) home run limit. Team 'A' has hit four and batter B4 hits a home run out of the ball park. He deliberately misses 2B and after all runs have scored, team 'B' appeals B4 for missing 2B. The umpire calls B4 out. Does the home run count towards the five limit? RULING: Yes. Whether the runner B4 intentionally or unintentionally missed 2B the home run would count. If the runner B4 missed 1B, the home run would not count, and if the third out of the inning, no runs would score.

PLAY (2) — Runner R1 on 2B with one out. Class 'A' slow pitch tournament with five (5) home run limitation. Team 'A' has hit four and batter B4 hits a long fly ball to F8 in centerfield. F8 catches the ball and throws it over the fence in order for team 'A' to have five home run limit. RULING: This would be a legal catch and if less than two out and other runners on base, the umpires should award all runners two bases for throwing the ball intentionally out of play. It would not count toward the home run limit.

RULE 6. PITCHING REGULATIONS (Fast Pitch)

Sec. 1. PRELIMINARIES. Before starting the delivery (pitch), the pitcher shall comply with the following:
a. He shall take a position with his pivot foot on the pitcher's plate and non-pivot foot on or behind the pitcher's plate. Both feet shall be on the ground within the 24 inch length of the pitcher's plate. His shoulders shall be in line with first and third bases. The hands shall be separated. The ball can be in the glove or pitching hand.
b. While in the position described in "a" above, he shall take the signal from the catcher.
c. After completing "b" above, he shall hold the ball in both hands for not less than one second and not more than 10 seconds before releasing the ball.

PLAY — Pitcher takes a signal while standing within eight feet of the pitcher's plate but not on the plate. He then assumes legal pitching position for one second and pitches the ball. RULING — Illegal pitch. The pitcher must take the signal while legally in contact with the pitcher's plate.

d. The pitcher shall not be considered in pitching position unless the catcher is in position to receive the pitch.
e. The pitcher may not take the pitching position on or near the pitcher's plate without having the ball in his possession.
NOTE: To indicate to the pitcher that he may not start the pitch, the umpire should raise one hand with the palm facing the pitcher. "NO PITCH" shall be declared if the pitcher pitches while the umpire has his hand in said position.

▶**Sec. 2. THE PITCH** starts when one hand is taken off the ball or the pitcher makes any motion that is part of his wind-up.
a. In the act of delivering the ball, the pitcher shall not take more than one step, which must be forward, toward the batter and simultaneously with the delivery of the ball to the batter. (Toward the batter is interpreted as within the 24 inch length of the pitcher's plate.)
▶b. Pushing off with the pivot foot from a place other than the pitcher's plate is illegal.
NOTE: It is not a step if the pitcher slides his foot across the pitcher's plate, provided contact is maintained with the pitcher's plate.

PLAY (1) — The pitcher stands on the right side of the pitcher's plate with both feet in legal contact. He takes a step with his non-pivot foot toward third base so that the entire foot lands to the right of the outside of the pitcher's plate. RULING — Illegal Pitch.

PLAY (2) — The pitcher stands with two feet on the pitching rubber and takes the signal. He then steps or slides back with the non-pivot foot (a) while his hands are separated, (b) while his hands are joined. RULING — (a) legal and (b) illegal. Because his step must be forward with the non-pivot foot, a step back must be completed prior to the start of the pitch as described in Rule 6, Section 2.

Sec. 3. A LEGAL DELIVERY SHALL BE A BALL WHICH IS DELIVERED TO THE BATTER WITH AN UNDERHANDED MOTION.
a. The release of the ball and follow through of the hand and wrist must be forward, past the straight line of the body.
b. The hand shall be below the hip, and the wrist not farther from the body than the elbow.
c. The pitch is completed with a step toward the batter.
d. The catcher must be within the lines of the catcher's box when the pitch is released.

PLAY — A pitch is delivered with the catcher outside the boundaries of the catcher's box. RULING — Illegal Pitch.

e. The catcher shall return the ball directly to the pitcher after each pitch, except a strikeout or putout made by the catcher.

EXCEPTION: Sec 3e does not apply when (a) a batter becomes a baserunner, (b) there are runners on base, or (c) a foul ball if fielded close to the foul line by the catcher who throws to first base for a possible out.

f. The pitcher has 20 second to release the next pitch after receiving the ball from the catcher.

PLAY — Bases are empty and the batter has a count of one strike and no balls. On the next pitch, the batter hits a foul ball which the catcher retrieves and throws to the third baseman. RULING — A ball is awarded to the batter and the count becomes two strikes and one ball.

Sec. 4. THE PITCHER MAY USE ANY WINDUP DESIRED, PROVIDING:
a. He does not make any motion to pitch without immediately delivering the ball to the batter.
b. He does not use a rocker action in which, after having the ball in both hands in the pitching position, he removes one hand from the ball, takes a backward and forward swing, and returns the ball to both hands in front of the body.
c. He does not use a windup in which there is a stop or reversal of the forward motion.
▶d. He does not make two revolution of the arm in the windmill pitch. A pitcher may drop his arm to the side and to the rear before starting the windmill motion.
e. He does not continue to wind up after taking the forward step, which is simultaneous with the release of the ball.

Sec. 5. THE PITCHER SHALL NOT DELIBERATELY DROP, ROLL OR BOUNCE THE BALL WHILE IN THE PITCHING POSITION IN ORDER TO PREVENT THE BATTER FROM STRIKING IT. A pitch out for the purpose of intentionally walking a batter is not considered an illegal pitch. (Refer to note following Rule 8, Sec 2c).

Sec. 6. THE PITCHER SHALL NOT, AT ANY TIME DURING THE GAME, BE ALLOWED TO USE TAPE OR ANY OTHER FOREIGN SUBSTANCES UPON THE BALL, THE PITCHING HAND OR FINGERS, NOR SHALL ANY OTHER PLAYER APPLY A FOREIGN SUBSTANCE TO THE BALL. Under the supervision and control of the umpire, powdered resin may be used to dry the hands. The pitcher shall not wear a sweatband, bracelet or similar type item on the wrist or forearm of the pitching arm.

Sec. 7. THE PITCHER SHALL NOT DELIVER A PITCH unless all defensive players, except the catcher who must be in the catcher's box, are positioned in fair territory.

▶NOTE: It is an illegal pitch if a fielder takes up a position in the batter's line of vision or, with deliberate unsportsmanlike intent, act in a manner to distract the batter. A pitch does not have to be released. The offended player shall be ejected from the game and an illegal pitch shall be declared.

EFFECT — Sec. 1-7: Any infraction of Sections 1-7 is an illegal pitch, with the exception of Section 3e, which is covered above. The ball is dead. A ball is called on the batter. Baserunners are entitled to advance one base without liability to be put out. If an illegal pitch hits the batter, the batter is awarded first base.
EXCEPTION: If the pitcher completes the delivery of the ball to the batter; and, if the batter hits the ball and reaches first base safely; and if all baserunners advance at least one base on the action resulting from the batted ball, the play stands and the illegal pitch is nullified. A delayed dead ball will be signified by the umpire extending his left arm horizontally.

NOTE: An illegal pitch shall be called immediately when it becomes illegal. If called by the plate umpire, it shall be called in a voice so that the catcher and the batter will hear it. The plate umpire will also give the delayed dead ball signal. If called by the base umpire, it shall be called so that the nearest fielder shall hear it. The base umpire shall also give the delayed dead ball signal. Failure of players to hear the call shall not void the call.

Sec. 8. AT THE BEGINNING OF EACH HALF INNING OR WHEN A PITCHER RELIEVES ANOTHER, NOT MORE THAN ONE MINUTE MAY BE USED TO DELIVER NOT MORE THAN FIVE PITCHES TO THE CATCHER OR OTHER TEAMMATE. Play shall be suspended during this time. For excessive warm-up pitches, a pitcher shall be penalized by awarding a ball to the batter for each pitch in excess of five.

PLAY — S1 replaces F1. How many throws are permitted for his warm-up? RULING — Five; however, the umpire is authorized to allow more throws when the weather is inclement or F1 was removed because of an injury and S1 did not have time to warm up before entering.

Sec. 9. THE PITCHER SHALL NOT THROW TO A BASE DURING A LIVE BALL WHILE HIS FOOT IS IN CONTACT WITH THE PITCHER'S PLATE AFTER HE HAS TAKEN THE PITCHING POSITION.
EFFECT — Sec. 9: Illegal pitch, the ball is dead, a ball is called on the batter and all runners advance one base. If the throw from the pitcher's plate is during a live ball appeal play, the appeal is cancelled.

NOTE: The pitcher can remove himself from the pitching position by stepping backwards off the pitcher's plate. Stepping forward or sideways constitutes an illegal pitch. It is an illegal pitch if a fielder takes up a position in the batter's line of vision or, with deliberate unsportsmanlike intent, act in a manner to distract the batter. A pitch does not have to be released.

Sec. 10. NO PITCH SHALL BE DECLARED WHEN:
a. The pitcher pitches during the suspension of play.
b. The pitcher attempts a quick return of the ball before the batter has taken position or is off balance as a result of a previous pitch.
c. The runner is called out for leaving the base prior to the pitcher releasing the pitch.
d. The pitcher pitches before a baserunner has retouched his base after a foul ball has been declared and the ball is dead.

EFFECT — Sec. 10a-d: The ball is dead and all subsequent action on that pitch is cancelled.

e. NO PLAYER, MANAGER OR COACH SHALL CALL "TIME," EMPLOY ANY OTHER WORD OR PHRASE, OR COMMIT ANY ACT WHILE THE BALL IS ALIVE AND IN PLAY FOR THE OBVIOUS PURPOSE OF TRYING TO MAKE THE PITCHER COMMIT AN ILLEGAL PITCH.

EFFECT — Sec. 10e: No pitch shall be declared and a warning issued to the offending team. A repeat of this type act by the team warned shall result in the offender being removed from the game.

PLAY — Pitcher is in his windup when the batter, in an attempt to have the pitcher commit an illegal pitch, raises his hand as if to request "time." Pitcher stops his windup. RULING — No pitch shall be declared.

Sec. 11. THERE SHALL BE ONLY ONE CHARGED CONFERENCE BETWEEN THE MANAGER OR OTHER TEAM REPRESENTATIVE FROM THE DUGOUT WITH EACH AND EVERY PITCHER IN AN INNING. The second charged conference shall result in the removal of the pitcher from the pitching position for the remainder of the game.

Sec. 12. IF THE BALL SLIPS FROM THE PITCHER'S HAND DURING HIS WINDUP OR DURING THE BACKSWING, THE BALL WILL BE IN PLAY AND THE RUNNERS MAY ADVANCE AT THEIR OWN RISK.

RULE 6. PITCHING REGULATIONS (Modified)

Modified rules are the same as regular fast pitch with the exception of Rule 6, Pitching.

THE FAST PITCH PITCHING RULES ARE IN EFFECT EXCEPT:
a. The pitcher must release the ball on the first forward swing of the pitching arm past the hip. The release must have a complete smooth follow through, with no abrupt stop of the arm near the hip.
b. The ball must not be outside the pitcher's wrist at the top of the backswing, and during the complete forward delivery.
c. The pitcher may take the ball behind the back on the backswing.
d. The pitcher may not use a windmill or slingshot type pitch, nor may a complete revolution be made in the delivery.
NOTE: A "slingshot" type pitch is defined as turning the body toward first or third base and, bending the elbow during the backswing.
e. The pitcher's palm may be pointing downward upon delivery.

RULE 6. PITCHING REGULATIONS (Slow Pitch)

Sec. 1. THE PITCHER SHALL TAKE A POSITION WITH BOTH FEET FIRMLY ON THE GROUND AND WITH ONE OR BOTH FEET IN CONTACT WITH, BUT NOT OFF THE SIDE OF, THE PITCHER'S PLATE. While the pivot foot is in contact with the pitcher's plate and throughout the delivery, both the pivot and non-pivot foot must be within the length of the pitcher's plate when on the ground or on the pitcher's plate.

Preliminary to pitching, the pitcher must come to a full and complete stop, with the ball in front of the body. The front of the body must face the batter.
a. *The front of the body must face the batter.*
b. This position must be maintained at least one second and not more than 10 seconds before starting the delivery.
c. The pitcher shall not be considered in pitching position unless the catcher is in position to receive the pitch.

NOTE: To indicate to the pitcher that he may not start the pitch, the umpire should raise one hand with the palm facing the pitcher. "NO PITCH" shall be declared if the pitcher pitches while the umpire has his hand in said position.

▶**Sec. 2. THE PITCH** starts when the pitcher makes any motion that is part of his windup after the required pause. Prior to the required pause, any windup may be used. The pivot foot must reamin in contact with the pitcher's plate until the pitched ball leaves the hand. *If a step is taken, it can be forward or BACKWARD, provided the foot is in contact with the pitching plate when the ball is released and the step is within the 24 inches (60.96cm) of the pitcher's plate and simultaneous with the release of the ball.*

PLAY — F1 has both feet on the rubber. F1 removes one foot by stepping backward and then pitches ball to B1. B1 does not swing at the pitch. RULING — Legal pitch. A step with the free foot is not required in slow pitch, but if one is taken, it can be forward or backward as long as the pivot foot remains in contact with the pitching plate until the ball is released.

Sec. 3. A LEGAL DELIVERY SHALL BE A BALL WHICH IS DELIVERED TO THE BATTER WITH AN UNDERHANDED MOTION.

PLAY (1) — The pitcher comes to a two-second stop, takes the ball in his pitching hand over the top of his head, down and around in a windmill type action, and releases the ball the first time past the hip. RULING — Legal. A windmill delivery is legal if the ball is released the first time past the hip and all other aspects of the pitching rule are followed.

PLAY (2) — The pitcher releases the ball during a pitch with his palm on top of the ball and with the ball facing the ground. RULING — Legal.

a. The pitch shall be released at a moderate speed. The speed is left entirely up to the umpire. The umpire shall warn the pitcher who delivers a pitch with excessive speed. If the pitcher repeats such an act after being warned, he shall be removed from the pitcher's position for the remainder of the game.

PLAY — After one warning, F1 again delivers a pitch with excessive speed. Plate umpire orders that F1 must be removed from the game. Manager attempts to change F1 to an outfield position but umpire rules that the pitcher cannot participate in any position for the remainder of the game. RULING — Illegal. F1 shall be removed from the pitching position for the remainder of the game but may participate in the game in any other position.

b. The hand shall be below the hip.
c. The ball must be delivered with a perceptible arc, and reach a height of at least six feet (1.83m) from the ground while not exceeding a maximum height of 12 feet (3.66m) from the ground.

PLAY — Pitcher releases ball in a pitch to the batter and the ball reaches a height of 15 feet before beginning its downward flight toward the plate. RULING — Illegal Pitch.

d. The catcher must be within the lines of the catcher's box until the pitched ball is batted or reaches the catcher's box.
e. The catcher shall return the ball directly to the pitcher after each pitch, except after a strikeout or putout made by the catcher.
f. The pitcher has 20 seconds to release the next pitch after receiving the ball from the catcher.

EFFECT — Sec. 3e: An additional "ball" is awarded to the batter.

PLAY — R1 on first base. Count on batter is one strike and no balls. Batter hits a foul ball which the catcher retrieves and gives the ball to the umpire. The umpire gives the catcher a new ball which he throws to the first baseman. RULING — A ball is awarded to the batter. In slow pitch, the rule applies regardless of whether or not runners are on base.

Sec. 4. THE PITCHER MAY USE ANY WINDUP DESIRED, PROVIDING:
a. He does not make any motion to pitch without immediately delivering the ball to the batter.
b. His windup is a continuous motion.
c. He does not use a windup in which there is a stop or reversal of the pitching motion.
d. He delivers the ball toward home plate on the first forward swing of the pitching arm past the hip.
e. He does not continue to wind up after he releases the ball.
f. He does not pitch the ball behind his back or between his legs.

Sec. 5. THE PITCHER SHALL NOT DELIBERATELY DROP, ROLL OR BOUNCE THE BALL WHILE IN THE PITCHING POSITION IN ORDER TO PREVENT THE BATTER FROM STRIKING IT.

Sec. 6. THE PITCHER SHALL NOT, AT ANY TIME DURING THE GAME, BE ALLOWED TO USE TAPE OR ANY OTHER FOREIGN SUBSTANCES UPON THE BALL, THE PITCHING HAND OR FINGERS, NOR SHALL ANY OTHER PLAYER APPLY A FOREIGN SUBSTANCE TO THE BALL. Under the supervision and control of the umpire, powdered resin may be used to dry the hands. The pitcher shall not wear a sweatband, bracelet or similar type item on the wrist or forearm of the pitching arm.

PLAY (1) — Pitcher with tape on pitching hand. RULING — Illegal. Must remove tape or be replaced.

PLAY (2) — The pitcher holding the ball in his glove hand, delivers the pitch from the glove hand. RULING — Illegal pitch. He must deliver the ball with his bare hand.

Sec. 7. AT THE BEGINNING OF EACH HALF INNING OR WHEN A PITCHER RELIEVES ANOTHER, NOT MORE THAN ONE MINUTE MAY BE USED TO DELIVER NOT MORE THAN FIVE PITCHES TO THE CATCHER OR OTHER TEAMMATE. Play shall be suspended during this time. For excessive warm-up pitches, a pitcher shall be penalized by awarding a ball to the batter for each pitch in excess of five.

Sec. 8. THE PITCHER SHALL NOT ATTEMPT A QUICK RETURN OF THE BALL BEFORE THE BATTER HAS TAKEN HIS POSITION OR IS OFF BALANCE AS A RESULT OF A PREVIOUS PITCH.

▶NOTE: It is an illegal pitch if a fielder takes up a position in the batter's line of vision or, with deliberate unsportsmanlike intent, act in a manner to distract the batter. A pitch does not have to be released. The offended player shall be ejected from the game and an illegal pitch shall be declared.

EFFECT — Sec. 1-8: Any infraction of Sections 1-8 is an illegal pitch. A ball shall be

called on the batter. Baserunners are not advanced.
EXCEPTION: If a batter strikes at any illegal pitch, it shall be a strike and there shall be no penalty for such an illegal pitch. The ball shall remain in play if hit by the batter. If an illegal pitch is called during an appeal play, the appeal is cancelled.

NOTE: An illegal pitch shall be called immediately when it becomes illegal. If called by the plate umpire, it shall be called in a voice so that the catcher and the batter will hear it. The plate umpire will also give the delayed dead ball signal. If called by the base umpire, it shall be called so that the nearest fielder shall hear it. The base umpire shall also give the delayed dead ball signal. Failure of players to hear the call shall not void the call.

Sec. 9. NO PITCH SHALL BE DECLARED WHEN:
a. The pitcher pitches during the suspension of play.
b. The runner is called out for leaving the base before the pitched ball reaches home plate.
c. The pitcher pitches before the baserunner has retouched his base after a foul ball has been declared and the ball is dead.
d. THE BALL SLIPS FROM THE PITCHER'S HAND DURING HIS WINDUP OR DURING THE BACKSWING.

EFFECT — Sec. 9a-d: The ball is dead and all subsequent action on that pitch is cancelled.

e. NO PLAYER, MANAGER OR COACH SHALL CALL "TIME," EMPLOY ANY OTHER WORD OR PHRASE, OR COMMIT ANY ACT WHILE THE BALL IS ALIVE AND IN PLAY FOR THE OBVIOUS PURPOSE OF TRYING TO MAKE THE PITCHER COMMIT AN ILLEGAL PITCH.

EFFECT — Sec. 9e: No pitch shall be declared and a warning issued to the offending team. A repeat of this type act by the team warned shall result in the offender being removed from the game.

PLAY — REFER TO RULE 6, SECTION 9e EFFECT (FAST PITCH).

Sec. 10. THERE SHALL BE ONLY ONE CHARGED CONFERENCE BETWEEN THE MANAGER OR OTHER TEAM REPRESENTATIVE FROM THE DUGOUT WITH EACH AND EVERY PITCHER IN AN INNING. The second charged conference shall result in the removal of the pitcher from the pitching position for the remainder of the game.

RULE 6. PITCHING REGULATIONS (16-Inch Slow Pitch)

Sec. 1. THE PITCHER SHALL TAKE A POSITION WITH BOTH FEET FIRMLY ON THE GROUND, AND WITH ONE OR BOTH FEET IN CONTACT WITH, BUT NOT OFF THE SIDE OF, THE PITCHER'S PLATE.
a. Preliminary to pitching, the pitcher must come to a full and complete stop facing the batter, with the shoulders in line with first and third bases and with the ball held in one or both hands in front of the body.
b. This position must be maintained at least one second and not more than 10 seconds before starting the delivery.
c. The pitcher shall not be considered in pitching position unless the catcher is in position to receive the pitch.

NOTE: To indicate to the pitcher that he may not start the pitch, the umpire should raise one hand with the palm facing the pitcher. "NO PITCH" shall be declared if the pitcher pitches while the umpire has his hand in said position.

Sec. 2. THE PITCH starts when the pitcher makes any motion that is part of his windup after the required pause. Prior to the required pause, any windup may be used. THE PIVOT FOOT MUST REMAIN IN CONTACT WITH THE PITCHER'S PLATE UNTIL THE PITCHED BALL LEAVES THE HAND. It is not necessary to step, but if a step is taken, it must be forward, toward the batter.

Sec. 3. A LEGAL DELIVERY SHALL BE A BALL WHICH IS DELIVERED TO THE BATTER WITH AN UNDERHANDED MOTION.
a. The pitch shall be released at a moderate speed. The speed is left entirely up to the umpire. The umpire shall warn the pitcher who delivers a pitch with excessive speed. If the pitcher repeats such an act after being warned, he shall be removed from the pitcher's position for the remainder of the game.
b. The hand shall be below the hip.
c. The ball must be delivered with a perceptible arc, and reach a height of at least six feet (1.83m) from the ground while not exceeding a maximum height of 12 feet (3.66m) from the ground.
d. The catcher must be within the lines of the catcher's box until the pitched ball is batted or reaches home plate.
e. The catcher shall return the ball directly to the pitcher after each pitch, except after a strikeout or putout made by the catcher. The pitcher has 20 seconds to release the next pitch.
EFFECT — Sec. 3e: An additional "ball" is awarded to the batter.

NOTE: Rule 6, Section 3e does not apply when a batter becomes a baserunner or when there are runners on base.

PLAY — *With R1 on third base, the catcher throws to F5 to pick off the runner after the pitch. (a) The runner R1 is tagged out, (b) the ball is overthrown and goes into left field. RULING — In (a) the runner R1 is out, and in (b) the ball is dead and R1 must return to third base.*

Sec. 4. THE PITCHER MAY USE TWO HESITATION PITCHES, IF HE SO DESIRES, BEFORE THE MANDATORY DELIVERY TO HOME PLATE. Except on a pick off by the pitcher, the pitcher may use any windup desired, providing:
a. His windup is a continuous motion.
b. He does not use a windup in which there is a stop or reversal of the forward motion.
c. He does not continue to wind up after he releases the ball.
d. He does not pitch the ball behind his back or between his legs.

▶NOTE: *A throw to a base is not considered a hesitation pitch, however a fake to a base is counted as a hesitation pitch.*

PLAY — *The pitcher (a) makes one hesitation pitch, throws to first base to try to pick off the runner and when the ball is returned, makes another hesitation pitch prior to pitching; (b) makes two hesitation pitches and as the runner takes off for 2B he walks off the pitcher's plate toward the runner; (c) makes two hesitation pitches and as the runner takes off for 2B, he steps back off the pitcher's plate and throws to 2B to pick off the runner; (d) on the throw to 1B to pick off the runner, the ball is overthrown and stays in play or goes out of play. RULING: (a) Legal, (b) Illegal pitch, (c) Legal and if the runner is tagged he will be out, (d) The ball is dead in either situation when the runner is not tagged and the runner remains at 1B.*

Sec. 5. THE PITCHER SHALL NOT DELIBERATELY DROP, ROLL OR BOUNCE THE BALL WHILE IN THE PITCHING POSITION IN ORDER TO PREVENT THE BATTER FROM STRIKING IT.

Sec. 6. THE PITCHER SHALL NOT, AT ANYTIME DURING THE GAME, BE ALLOWED TO USE TAPE OR OTHER SUBSTANCES UPON THE BALL, THE PITCHING HAND OR FINGERS, NOR SHALL ANY OTHER PLAYER APPLY A FOREIGN SUBSTANCE TO THE BALL. Under the supervision and control of the umpire, powdered resin may be used to dry the hands. The pitcher shall not wear a sweatband, bracelet or similar type item on the wrist or forearm of the pitching arm.

Sec. 7. AT THE BEGINNING OF EACH HALF INNING OR WHEN A PITCHER RELIEVES ANOTHER, NOT MORE THAN ONE MINUTE MAY BE USED TO DELIVER NOT MORE THAN FIVE PITCHES TO THE CATCHER OR OTHER TEAMMATE. Play shall be suspended during this time. For excessive warm-up pitches, a pitcher shall be penalized by awarding a ball to the batter for each pitch in excess of five.

Sec. 8. THE PITCHER MAY ATTEMPT TO PICK A RUNNER OFF BASE EVEN WHILE HIS FOOT IS IN CONTACT WITH THE PITCHER'S PLATE. As stated in Rule 6, Section 4, the pitcher is allowed only two hesitation pitches.

EFFECT — Sec. 1-8: Any infraction of Sections 1-8 is an illegal pitch and the ball is dead. A ball shall be called on the batter and baserunners do not advance.
EXCEPTION: If a batter strikes at any illegal pitch, it shall be a strike and there shall be no penalty for such an illegal pitch. The ball shall remain in play if hit by the batter. If an illegal pitch is called during an appeal play, the appeal is cancelled.

NOTE: An illegal pitch shall be called when it becomes illegal. If called by the plate umpire, it shall be called in a voice so that the catcher and batter will hear it. The plate umpire will also give the delayed dead ball signal. If called by the base umpire, it shall be called so that the nearest fielder shall hear it. The base umpire shall also give the delayed dead ball signal. Failure of players to hear the call shall not void the call.

It is an illegal pitch if a fielder takes a position in the batter's line of vision or, with deliberate unsportsmanlike intent, acts in a manner to distract the batter. A pitch does not have to be released.

Sec. 9. NO PITCH SHALL BE DECLARED WHEN:
a. The pitcher pitches during the suspension of play.
b. The pitcher attempts a quick return of the ball before the batter has taken his position or is off balance as a result of a previous pitch.
c. The pitcher pitches before the baserunner has retouched his base after a foul ball has been declared and the ball is dead.
EFFECT — Sec. 9a-c: The ball is dead and all subsequent action on that pitch is cancelled.
d. NO PLAYER, MANAGER OR COACH SHALL CALL "TIME," EMPLOY ANY OTHER WORD OR PHRASE, OR COMMIT ANY ACT WHILE THE BALL IS ALIVE AND IN PLAY FOR THE OBVIOUS PURPOSE OF TRYING TO MAKE THE PITCHER COMMIT AN ILLEGAL PITCH.
EFFECT — Sec. 9d: No pitch shall be declared and a warning issued to the offending team. A repeat of this type act by the team warned shall result in the offender being removed from the game.

Sec. 10. THERE SHALL BE ONLY ONE CHARGED CONFERENCE BETWEEN THE MANAGER OR OTHER TEAM REPRESENTATIVE FROM THE DUGOUT WITH EACH AND EVERY PITCHER IN AN INNING. The second charged conference shall result in the removal of the pitcher from the pitching position for the remainder of the game.

Sec. 11. IF THE BALL SLIPS FROM THE PITCHER'S HAND DURING HIS WINDUP OR DURING THE BACKSWING, THE BALL WILL BE IN PLAY.

RULE 7. BATTING

Sec. 1. THE BATTER SHALL TAKE HIS POSITION WITHIN THE LINES OF THE BATTER'S BOX.
a. The batter shall not have his entire foot touching the ground completely outside the lines of the batter's box or touching home plate when the ball is hit.
b. The batter shall not step directly across in front of the catcher to the other batter's box while the pitcher is in position, ready to pitch.
c. The batter shall not enter the batter's box with an illegal bat.

PLAY — *Batter hits ball for a single with a bat 35 inches long. RULING — Illegal bat. Batter is called out and runners return if on base.*

EFFECT — Sec. 1a-c: The ball is dead, the batter is out, and baserunners may NOT advance.

d. The batter shall not enter the batter's box with an altered bat.
EFFECT — Sec. 1d: The ball is dead; the batter is out and, without warning, is remov-

ed from further participation in the game; and baserunners may not advance.

PLAY — REFER TO RULE 1, SECTION 1.

e. The batter must take his position within 20 seconds after the umpire has called "play ball."
EFFECT — Sec. 1e: The ball is dead. The batter is out.
f. The batter must have both feet completely within the lines of the batter's box prior to the start of the pitch. He may touch the lines, but no part of his foot may be outside of the lines prior to the pitch.

NOTE: The umpire should hold up the pitch until the batter is within the lines.

Sec. 2. EACH PLAYER OF THE SIDE AT BAT SHALL BECOME A BATTER IN THE ORDER IN WHICH HIS NAME APPEARS ON THE SCORESHEET.
a. The batting order of each team must be on the scoresheet and must be delivered before the game by the manager or captain to the plate umpire. The plate umpire shall submit it to the inspection of the manager or captain of the opposing team.
b. The batting order delivered to the umpire must be followed throughout the game unless a player is substituted. When this occurs, the substitute must take the place of the removed player in the batting order.
c. The first batter in each inning shall be the batter whose name follows that of the last player who completed a turn at bat in the preceding inning.
EFFECT — Sec. 2b-c: Batting out of order is an appeal play which may be made by the manager, player or coach of the defensive team only. The defensive team forfeits its right to appeal batting out of order when all infielders (including the pitcher) have left their normal positions (crossed the foul line).
  (1) If the error is discovered while the incorrect batter is at bat, the correct batter may take his place and legally assume any balls and strikes. Any runs scored or bases run while the incorrect batter was at bat shall be legal.
  (2) If the error is discovered after the incorrect batter has completed his turn at bat and before there has been a pitch to another batter, the player who should have batted is out. Any advance or score made because of a ball batted by the improper batter or because of the improper batter's advance to first base on a hit, an error, a base on balls or a hit batter shall be nullified. The next batter is the player whose name follows that of the player called out for failing to bat. If the batter declared out under these circumstances is the third out, the correct batter in the next inning shall be the player who would have come to bat had the player been put out by ordinary play.
  (3) If the error is discovered after the first pitch to the next batter, the turn at bat of the incorrect batter is legal, all runs scored and bases run are legal, and the next batter in order shall be the one whose name follows that of the incorrect batter. No one is called out for failure to bat. Players who have not batted and who have not been called out have lost their turn at bat until reached again in the regular order.
  (4) No baserunner shall be removed from the base he is occupying. (Except the batter-baserunner who has been taken off the base by the umpire as in (2) above to bat in his proper place.) He merely misses his turn at bat with no penalty. The batter following him in the batting order becomes the legal batter.

PLAY — With R1 on first, B7 is next on the batting list, but B8 erroneously takes his place. The error is discovered by opposing team personnel and reported to the umpire or official scorekeeper (a) after B8 has received two strikes, (b) after B8 has received a base on balls, (c) after B8 has had a foul which is caught or has made a safe hit to advance R1, (d) R1 is forced out at 2B and B8 is on first base, (e) after a pitch has been delivered to B9. RULING — In (a) B8 is replaced by B7 who assumes the two ball, two strike count; also, any advancement by R1 on first is legal. In (b) and (c), B7 is out. B8 is removed from base and bats again with no balls or strikes. R1 must return to first. In (d) B7 is out, return R1 to first, remove B8 from first and B8 bats again with no balls and strikes. In (e) no correction is made, and B7 and B8 do not bat again until their regular time.

d. When the third out in an inning is made before the batter has completed his turn at bat, he shall be the first batter in the next inning, and the ball and strike count on him shall be canceled.
e. The batting order for Co-Ed softball shall alternate the sexes. There are no exceptions to this rule.

PLAY (1) — In a Co-Ed game, Team "A" uses six male and four female players for the first three innings. It is detected by the umpire in the fourth inning. RULING: This is a violation of Rule 4, Section 6e, and the game is forfeited.

PLAY (2) — In a Co-Ed game, Team "B" lists a male player B8 following another male player B7 in the lineup and the scorebook. Prior to B8 batting his first time, and immediately after B7 bats the first time, the umpire notices the error in the batting order. RULING: Since the actual infraction has not occurred, the umpire should replace B8 with B9 (a female player) and continue the game.

PLAY (3) — Same as PLAY 2, except the detection of the irregularity is not made until after B7 and B8 have batted (one pitch to B8 is considered as B8 batting). RULING: The game shall be forfeited.

Sec. 3. THE BATTER SHALL NOT HINDER THE CATCHER FROM FIELDING OR THROWING THE BALL BY STEPPING OUT OF THE BATTER'S BOX OR INTENTIONALLY HINDER THE CATCHER WHILE STANDING WITHIN THE BATTER'S BOX.
►*EFFECT — Sec. 3: The ball is dead, the batter is out, and baserunners must return to the last base that, in the judgement of the umpire, was touched at the time of the interference.*

PLAY — (FP ONLY) With R1 going to third, B4 steps across home plate to hinder F2 who is fielding the ball or throwing to third. RULING — If R1 is tagged out despite the hindrance, the interference is ignored. If the runner is not tagged out, batter is declared out. The ball becomes dead immediately and all runners must return to base occupied at time of pitch.

Sec. 4. MEMBERS OF THE TEAM AT BAT SHALL NOT INTERFERE WITH A PLAYER ATTEMPTING TO FIELD A FOUL FLY BALL.

EFFECT — Sec. 4: The ball is dead, the batter is out, and baserunners must return to the base legally held at the time of the pitch.

Sec. 5: THE BATTER SHALL NOT HIT A FAIR BALL WITH THE BAT A SECOND TIME IN FAIR TERRITORY.
NOTE: If the batter drops the bat and the ball rolls against the bat in fair territory and, in the umpire's judgement, there was not intention to interfere with the course of the ball, the batter is not out and the ball is alive and in play.

EFFECT — Sec. 5: The ball is dead, the batter is out, and baserunners may not advance.

Sec. 6. A STRIKE IS CALLED BY THE UMPIRE:
a. (FP ONLY) For each legally pitched ball entering the strike zone before touching the ground and at which the batter does not swing.
EFFECT — Sec. 6a: (FP ONLY) The ball is in play and the baserunners may advance with liability to be put out.
(SP ONLY) For each legally pitched ball entering the strike zone before touching the ground and at which the batter does not swing. It is not a strike if the pitched ball touches home plate and is not swung at.
EFFECT — Sec. 6a: (SP ONLY) The ball is dead.
b. (FP ONLY) For each legally pitched ball struck at and missed by the batter.
EFFECT — Sec. 6b: (FP ONLY) The ball is in play and the baserunners may advance with liability to be put out.
(SP ONLY) For each pitched ball struck at and missed by the batter.
EFFECT — Sec. 6b: (SP ONLY) The ball is dead.
c. For each foul tip held by the catcher.
EFFECT — Sec. 6c: (FP ONLY) The ball is in play and baserunners may advance with liability to be put out. The batter is out if it is the third strike.
EFFECT — Sec. 6c: (SP ONLY) The batter is out if it is the third strike. The ball is dead on any strike.
(16-inch SP ONLY) For each foul tip.
d. (FP ONLY) For each foul ball not legally caught on the fly when the batter has less than two strikes.
(SP ONLY) For each foul ball not legally caught, including the third strike.
e. For each pitched ball struck at and missed which touches any part of the batter.

PLAY — On third strike, B3 strikes at and misses a pitch. Ball strikes his arm or person. RULING — B3 is out. Ball becomes dead.

f. When any part of the batter's person is hit with his own batted ball when he is in the batter's box and he has less than two strikes.
g. When a delivered ball by the pitcher hits the batter while the ball is in the strike zone.
EFFECT — Sec. 6d-g: The ball is dead and baserunners must return to their bases without liability to be put out.

Sec. 7. A BALL IS CALLED BY THE UMPIRE:
►a. For each legally pitched ball which does not enter the strike zone, touches the ground before reaching home plate, or touches home plate and at which the batter does not swing.
EFFECT — Sec. 7a: (FP ONLY) The ball is in play and baserunners are entitled to advance with liability to be put out.
EFFECT — Sec. 7a: (SP ONLY) The ball is dead. Baserunners may not advance.
b. (FP ONLY) For each illegally pitched ball.
EFFECT — Sec. 7b: (FP ONLY) The ball is dead and baserunners are entitled to advance one base without liability to be put out.
(SP ONLY) For each illegally pitched ball.
EFFECT — Sec. 7b: (SP ONLY) The ball is dead. Baserunners may not advance.
EXCEPTION: If the batter swings at the illegal pitch, the illegal pitch is ignored.
c. (SP ONLY) When a delivered ball by the pitcher hits the batsman outside of the strike zone.
d. When the catcher fails to return the ball directly to the pitcher as required in Rule 6, Section 3e.
e. When the pitcher fails to pitch the ball within 20 seconds.
f. For each excessive warm-up pitch.
EFFECT — Sec. 7c-f: The ball is dead. Baserunners may not advance.

Sec. 8. A FAIR BALL IS A LEGALLY BATTED BALL WHICH:
a. Settles or is touched on fair territory between home and first base or between home and third base.

PLAY — Batted ball first hits home plate and, without touching any foreign object, settles on fair ground between the pitcher's plate and home plate. RULING — Fair Ball.

b. Bounds past first or third base on or over fair territory.
c. While on or over fair territory, touches the person, attached equipment or clothing of a player or an umpire.
d. Touches first, second or third base.
e. First falls or is first touched on or over fair territory beyond first, second or third base.
EFFECT — Sec. 8a-e: The ball is in play and baserunners are entitled to advance any number of bases with liability to be put out. The batter becomes a baserunner unless the infield fly rule applies.
f. Over fair territory, passes out of the playing field beyond the outfield fence.
NOTE: If the ball hits the foul line pole above the fence level, it shall be a home run.

Sec. 9. A FOUL BALL IS A LEGALLY BATTED BALL WHICH:
a. Settles on foul territory between home and first base, or between home and third base.
b. Bounds past first or third base on or over foul territory.
c. While on or over foul territory, touches the person, attached equipment, or clothing of a player or umpire or any object foreign to the natural ground.
d. First falls or is first touched over foul territory beyond first or third base.
e. Touches the batter while the ball is within the batter's box.
f. Hits the bat in the batter's hand while within the batter's box.
EFFECT — Sec. 9a-f.
(1) The ball is dead unless it is a legally caught foul fly. If a foul fly is caught, the batter is out.
(2) (FP ONLY) A strike is called on the batter, unless he already has two strikes.
(SP ONLY) A strike is called on the batter for each foul ball not legally caught,

including the third strike.
(3) Baserunners must return to their bases without liability to be put out, unless a foul fly is caught. In this case, the baserunner may advance with liability to be put out after the ball has been touched.

Sec. 10. A FOUL TIP IS A BATTED BALL WHICH GOES DIRECTLY FROM THE BAT, NOT HIGHER THAN THE BATTER'S HEAD, TO THE CATCHER'S HANDS AND IS LEGALLY CAUGHT BY THE CATCHER.

NOTE: It is not a foul tip unless caught and any foul tip that is caught is a strike. In fast pitch, modified and 16-inch slow pitch, the ball is in play. In slow pitch, the ball is dead.

EFFECT — Sec. 10: (FP ONLY) A strike is called, the ball remains in play and baserunners may advance with liability to be put out.

EFFECT — Sec. 10: (SP ONLY) A strike is called; the ball is dead.

Sec. 11. THE BATTER IS OUT:
a. When the third strike is struck at, missed and the ball touches any part of the batter's person.
b. When a batter appears in the batter's box with or is discovered using an altered bat. The batter is also ejected from the game.
c. When the batter enters the batter's box with an illegal bat or is discovered using an illegal bat.

PLAY — REFER TO RULE 1, SECTION 1.

d. When a fly ball is legally caught.
e. Immediately when he hits an infield fly, as declared by the umpire, with runners on first and second or on first, second and third with less than two outs. This is called the INFIELD FLY RULE.

PLAY (1) — Umpire calls "infield fly" but ball curves to foul area. RULING — Announcement is reversed. It is not an infield fly but an ordinary foul. Batter is not out unless foul is caught. If caught, each runner must retouch his base before advancing.

PLAY (2) — REFER TO RULE 1, SECTION 36.

f. If a fielder intentionally drops a fair fly ball, including a line drive (FP or SP) or a bunt (FP ONLY), which can be caught by an infielder with ordinary effort with first, first and second, first and third or first, second and third bases occupied with less than two outs.

NOTE: A trapped ball shall not be considered as having been intentionally dropped.

EFFECT — Sec. 11f: The ball is dead and baserunners must return to the last base touched at the time of the pitch.

PLAY — With one out and R1 on first, B3 hits fly. F4 gets the ball in his hands but intentionally drops it for an attempted double play. RULING — Umpire should immediately announce B3 is out. Ball is dead. Baserunners may not advance.

g. If a preceding runner who is not yet out, in the umpire's judgement, intentionally interferes with a fielder who is attempting to catch a thrown ball or throw a ball in an attempt to complete the play. The runner shall also be called out and interference called.
h. (FP ONLY) When a called or swinging third strike is caught by the catcher.
i. (FP ONLY) When he has three strikes if there are less than two outs and first base is occupied.
j. (FP ONLY) When he bunts foul after the second strike. If the ball is caught in the air, it remains alive and in play.
k. (SP Only) After a third strike, including an uncaught foul ball that is hit after two strikes.
EXCEPTION: This rule does not apply in Junior Olympic youth slow pitch play.
l. (SP ONLY) When he bunts or chops the ball downward.

PLAY — (SP Only) R1 on second. B2 chops down on a pitched ball. F1 throws out R1 advancing to third. RULING — B2 is out for chopping down on the ball. Dead ball. R1 is returned to second.

Sec. 12. THE BATTER OR BASERUNNER IS NOT OUT IF A FIELDER MAKING A PLAY ON HIM USES AN ILLEGAL GLOVE. The manager of the offended team has the option of having the batter bat again and assuming the ball and strike count he had prior to the pitch he hit, or taking the result of the play.

PLAY — B1 hits a fly ball to F9. Umpire notices that F9 caught the ball with a first baseman's mitt. RULING — Remove the illegal piece of equipment from the game. Manager of the offended team is given the option of having the entire play nullified and batter bat over, assuming the ball and strike count before the pitch he hit, or accepting the play and disregarding the illegal catch.

Sec. 13. ON-DECK BATTER.
a. The on-deck batter is the offensive player whose name follows the name of the batter in the batting order.
b. The on-deck batter shall take a position within the lines of the on-deck circle nearest his bench.
c. The on-deck batter may loosen up with no more than two official softball bats, an approved warm-up bat, or a combination of the two — not to exceed two. Nothing such as a donut, fan, etc. may be attached to a bat when loosening up.
d. The on-deck batter may leave the on-deck circle:
(1) When he becomes the batter.
(2) To direct baserunners advancing from third to home plate.
e. When the on-deck batter interferes with the defensive player's opportunity to make a play on a runner, the runner closest to home plate at the time of the interference shall be declared out.
f. The provision of Rule 7, Section 4, shall apply to the on-deck batter.

RULE 8. BASERUNNING

Sec. 1. THE BASERUNNERS MUST TOUCH BASES IN LEGAL ORDER (i.e. FIRST, SECOND, THIRD AND HOME PLATE).
a. When a baserunner must return to bases while the ball is in play, he must touch the bases in reverse order.
EFFECT — Sec. 1a: The ball is in play and baserunners must return with liability to be put out.
b. When a baserunner acquires the right to a base by touching it before being put out, he is entitled to hold the base until he has legally touched the next base in order, or is forced to vacate it for a succeeding baserunner.
c. When a baserunner dislodges a base from its proper position, neither he nor the succeeding runners in the same series of plays are compelled to follow a base unreasonably out of position.
EFFECT — Sec. 1b-c: The ball is in play and baserunners may advance with liability to be put out.
d. A baserunner shall not run bases in reverse order either to confuse the fielders or to make a travesty of the game.
EFFECT — Sec. 1d: The ball is dead and the baserunner is out.
e. Two baserunners may not occupy the same base simultaneously.
EFFECT — Sec. 1e: The runner who first legally occupied the base shall be entitled to it. The other baserunner may be put out by being touched with the ball.
f. Failure of PRECEDING runner to touch a base legally on a caught fly ball and who is declared out does not affect the status of a SUCCEEDING baserunner who touches bases in proper order. However, if the failure to touch a base in regular order or to leave a base legally on a caught fly ball is the third out of the inning, NO SUCCEEDING runner may score a run.

PLAY — REFER TO RULE 5, SECTION 7.

g. No runner may return to touch a missed base or one he had left illegally after a following runner has scored.
h. No runner may return to touch a missed base or a base left too soon if he has advanced, touched, and remains a base beyond the missed base or the base left illegally, when the ball becomes dead.
i. No runner may return to touch a missed base or one he had left illegally once he enters his team dugout or bench area.
j. When a walk is issued, all runners must touch all bases in legal order.

PLAY — In the last of the seventh inning with the score tied, two outs, and bases full, B6 receives a walk to force R1 at home plate. Because B6 assumes that game is over, he fails to go to first and leaves the field. RULING — B6 is out, run does not count.

k. Bases left too soon on a caught fly ball must be retouched prior to advancing to awarded bases.
l. Awarded bases must also be touched in proper order.

Sec. 2. THE BATTER BECOMES A BATTER-BASERUNNER:
a. As soon as he hits a fair ball.
b. (FP ONLY) When the catcher fails to catch the third strike before the ball touches the ground when there are less than two outs and first base is unoccupied or anytime there are two outs. This is called the third strike rule.

PLAY — B1 has two strikes. The next pitch touches the ground in front of home plate and bounces through the strike zone. B1 swings at the pitch and F2 secures the ball in his mitt after the first bounce. B1 advances to first base while F2 holds the ball. RULING — This is the dropped third strike rule. The batter is not out and, if he beats the throw to first, he is also safe.

EFFECT — Sec. 2a-b: The ball is in play and the batter becomes a batter-baserunner with liability to be put out.

c. When four balls have been called by the umpire.
EFFECT — Sec. 2c (FP ONLY) The ball is in play unless it has been blocked. The batter is entitled to one base without liability to be put out.
NOTE: If the pitcher desires to walk a batter intentionally, all defensive players, except the catcher who must be in the catcher's box, must be positioned in fair territory. If the defense do not position themselves in fair territory, the umpire should call an illegal pitch when the pitch is thrown. See Rule 4, Section 2 NOTE and Rule 6, Section 7 EFFECT.

EFFECT — Sec. 2c: (SP ONLY) The ball is dead. Baserunners may not advance unless forced. If the pitcher desires to walk a batter intentionally, he may do so by notifying the plate umpire who shall award the batter first base. If two batters are to be walked intentionally, the second cannot be administered until the first reaches first base. NOTE: The awards must be made in order, not two at one time.
EFFECT — Sec. 2c: (Co-Ed) The ball is dead. On any walk to a male batter (intentional or not), the next batter — a female — has her choice of walking or hitting, up until the time she steps into the batter's box.
d. When the catcher obstructs or any other fielder interferes with or prevents him from striking at a pitched ball.
EFFECT — Sec. 2d: The ball is dead. The batter is awarded first base. Baserunners may not advance unless forced.
(1) The umpire shall give a "delayed dead ball signal."
(2) The manager of the batting team has the option of taking the award for "catcher obstruction" as described above, or he may take the result of the play.
(3) If the batter hits the ball and reaches first base safely, and if all other runners have advanced at least one base on the batted ball, catcher obstruction is cancelled. All actions as a result of the batted ball stand. No option is given.

PLAY — R1 on first base. The catcher touches the batter's bat prior to or during the swing. Batted ball is grounded to F6, who forces R1 at second base. B2 reaches first base safely. RULING — Since R1 did not advance at least one base, obstruction is called and the play is cancelled. R1 is awarded second base and B2 is awarded first base.

e. When a fair ball strikes the person or clothing of the umpire or a baserunner on fair ground.

► EFFECT — Sec. 2e: If the ball hits the umpire or baserunner (a) after touching a fielder, the ball is in play; (b) after passing a fielder other than the pitcher, the ball is in play; or (c) before passing a fielder without being touched, the ball is dead. If the baserunner is hit, he is out and the batter is entitled to first base without liability to be put out. Baserunners not forced by the batter-runner must return to the base they had reached prior to the interference.

PLAY — *With R1 on third and R2 on first, a ball batted by B3 strikes umpire who is: (a) on fair territory behind third baseman, or (b) behind the pitcher but in front of a baseman. RULING — In (a), ball remains alive since it has passed a fielder. In (b), unless ball touches F1, it becomes dead and each runner is sent to the base he occupied or to which he was being forced when the ball became dead (i.e. R1 remains on third, and R2 and B3 go to second and first).*

f. (FP ONLY) When a pitched ball, not struck at or not called a strike, touches any part of the batter's person or clothing while he is in the batter's box. It does not matter if the ball strikes the ground before hitting him. The batter's hands are not to be considered as part of the bat.
EFFECT — Sec. 2f: The ball is dead and the batter is entitled to one base without liability to be put out unless he made no effort to avoid being hit. In this case, the plate umpire calls either a ball or a strike.

Sec. 3. BASERUNNERS ARE ENTITLED TO ADVANCE WITH LIABILITY TO BE PUT OUT:

a. (FP ONLY) On the pitcher's delivery, when the ball leaves the pitcher's hand.
b. When the ball is thrown into fair or foul territory and is not blocked.
c. When the ball is batted into fair territory and is not blocked.
d. When a legally caught fly ball is first touched.
e. If a fair ball strikes the umpire or a baserunner after having passed an infielder, other than the pitcher, or having been touched by an infielder, including the pitcher, the ball shall be considered in play.
EFFECT — Sec. 3a-e: The ball is alive and in play.

Sec. 4. A PLAYER FORFEITS HIS EXEMPTION FROM LIABILITY TO BE PUT OUT:

a. If, while the ball is in play, he fails to touch the base to which he was entitled before attempting to make the next base. If the runner put out is the batter- baserunner at first base or any other baserunner forced to advance because the batter became a baserunner, this out is a force-out.
b. If, after overrunning first base, the batter-baserunner attempts to continue to second base.
c. If, after dislodging the base, the batter-baserunner tries to continue to the next base.
d. (16-inch SP ONLY) A player may lead off from any base with a risk of being picked off by a throw from the pitcher or catcher. If a throw from the pitcher or catcher results in an overthrown or blocked ball, no runners may advance. Any runner advancing on a pitch not hit is liable to be put out if tagged before returning to the runner's original base.

PLAY — *R1 leads off first base and advances to second on the pitch. The ball is thrown by F2 to F4, who tags R1 while R1 is standing on second base. RULING — R1 is out. He may lead off, but must return to his base before being tagged if the ball is not hit.*

Sec. 5. BASERUNNERS ARE ENTITLED TO ADVANCE WITHOUT LIABILITY TO BE PUT OUT:

a. When forced to vacate a base because the batter was awarded a base on balls.
EFFECT — Sec. 5a: (FP ONLY) The ball remains in play unless it is blocked. Baserunner affected is entitled to one base and may advance further at his own risk if the ball is in play.
EFFECT — Sec. 5a: (SP ONLY) The ball is dead.
b. When a fielder obstructs the baserunner from making a base, unless the fielder is trying to field a batted ball, has the ball ready to touch the baserunner, or is about to receive a thrown ball.
EFFECT — Sec. 5b: When obstruction occurs, the umpire will call and signal obstruction.
(1) If a play is being made on the obstructed runner or if the batter-baserunner is obstructed before he touches first base, the ball is dead and all runners shall advance, without liability to be put out, to the bases they would have reached, in the umpire's judgement, if there had been no obstruction.
EXCEPTION: A baserunner obstructed in a rundown shall be awarded one base beyond the base last touched at the time of the obstruction regardless of the direction of the runner. Any preceding runners forced to advance by the award of bases as the penalty for obstruction shall advance without liability to be put out.
(2) If no play is being made on the obstructed runner at the time of obstruction, the play shall proceed until the next play is completed or the obstructed runner is played upon. The umpire will then call "time" and impose such penalties, if any, that will nullify the act of obstruction. If, in the judgement of the umpire, the obstructed runner a) would have reached the base he was played on, he will be awarded that base; b) is put out prior to reaching the next base after the obstruction, and in the judgement of the umpire, he would not have reached that base, the runner is returned to the last base touched at the time of the obstruction; or c) goes beyond the base that he would have reached had he not been obstructed, the runner runs at his own risk and my be put out.
(3) When a runner is obstructed while advancing or returning to a base by a fielder who neither has the ball nor is attempting to field a batted ball, or a fielder without the ball fakes a tag, the umpire shall award the obstructed runner and each other runner affected by the obstruction, the bases they would have reached, in his judgement, had there been no obstruction. If the umpire feels there is justification, a defensive player making a fake tag could be removed from the game.

►NOTE: Obstructed baserunners are still required to touch all bases in proper order or could be called out on a proper appeal by the defensive team.

(4) Catcher obstruction is covered under Rule 8, Section 2d.

PLAY (1) — *With R1 on third and R2 on second, R1 is caught between third and home. As R1 is attempting to regain third, F5 obstructs R1. RULING — The umpire should call "obstruction." R1 should be awarded home. R2 is permitted to return to second base.*

PLAY (2) — *The ball is hit to F9. As R1 passes first base, he is obstructed while no play is being made on him. he is thrown out by a wide margin at home plate. RULING — If, in the judgement of the umpire, R1 advanced beyond the base he would have made had he not been obstructed, he is out.*

c. (FP ONLY) When a wild pitch or passed ball goes under, over, through or lodges in the backstop.
EFFECT — Sec. 5c: The ball is dead. All baserunners are awarded one base only. The batter is awarded first base only on the fourth ball.
d. When forced to vacate a base because the batter was awarded a base.
(1) (FP ONLY) For being hit by a pitched ball.
(2) For being obstructed by the catcher when striking at a pitched ball.
EFFECT — Sec. 5d (1)-(2): The ball is dead and baserunners may not advance farther than the base to which they are entitled.
(3) (FP ONLY) If, with a runner on third base and trying to score by means of a squeeze play or a steal, the catcher or any other fielder steps on or in front of home plate without possession of the ball or touches the batter or his bat, the pitcher shall be charged with an illegal pitch, the batter shall be awarded first base on the interference and the ball is dead.

PLAY — *R1 is on third base. A squeeze play is in progress as the batter attempts to bunt the pitched ball and is interfered with by the catcher. RULING — Illegal pitch and interference is declared. R1 is awarded home plate and batter is awarded first base.*

e. (FP ONLY) When a pitcher makes an illegal pitch.
EFFECT — Sec. 5e: The ball is dead and baserunners may advance to the base to which they are entitled without liability to be put out.
f. When a fielder contacts or catches a fair batted or thrown ball with his cap, mask, glove or any part of his uniform while it is detached from its proper place on his person.
EFFECT — Sec. 5f: The baserunners would be entitled to three bases if a batted ball or two bases if a thrown ball; and in either case, the baserunners may advance further at their own risk. If the illegal catch or touch is made on a fair hit ball which, in the judgement of the umpire, would have cleared the outfield fence in flight, the runner shall be awarded a home run.

PLAY — *R1 is on second and R2 is on first when B3 hits ground ball to F6. F6 fields the ball, steps on second for a force on R2, advancing from first, then throws wildly to F3. F3 tosses his mitt into the air striking the ball. The ball bounces into the dugout. RULING — R2 is out. Both R1 and B3 are awarded two bases each from their position when the detached mitt of F3 touched the thrown ball. In this situation or any other situation where detached glove or mitt touches a ball, prior to the ball becoming dead because of going into a dead ball area, the rule which applies to detached player equipment prevails. If the detached glove or mitt touches the ball after the ball has become dead by going into a dead ball area, the ruling governing detached player equipment has no bearing.*

g. *When the ball is in play and is overthrown (beyond the boundary lines) or is blocked.*
EFFECT — Sec 5g. All runners will be awarded two bases and the award will be governed by the position of the runners when the ball left any fielder's hand.
EXCEPTION: When a fielder loses possession of the ball, such as on an attempted tag, and the ball enters the dead ball area or becomes blocked, all runners are awarded one base from the last base touched at the time the ball entered the dead ball area or became blocked. If a runner touches the next base and returns to his original base, the original base he left is considered the "last base touched" for purposes of an overthrow award.

PLAY (1) — *R1 and R2 are on second and first bases respectively. B3 hits the ball to F6, who muffs the ball, recovers it, then throws late to F3 in an attempt to retire B3. R1 and R2 reach third and second bases respectively. R1 attempts to advance to home, thereby drawing a throw from F3 which goes into the dugout. RULING — R1 and R2 are awarded home and B3 is awarded third.*

PLAY (2) — *R1 on first. B2 hits ground ball to F6. F6 flips the ball to F4 for force out on R1. Relay to F3 from F4 goes into the dugout area. B2 has already passed first base before relay is ¨ade. RULING — B2 is awarded third base. Award of bases is governed by the position of each runner and the last base he has touched at the time of the throw.*

PLAY (3) — *No runners on base. B1 hits ball to F10, who throws ball to F3 to force out B1. B1 is already past first base when ball is released by F10. The ball bounces past F3 and into the stands. RULING — B1 is awarded third base.*

PLAY (4) — *A thrown ball hits a bat or glove lying on the ground (other than the bat discarded by the batter). RULING — (1) If the bat or glove belongs to the team at bat, it is ruled interference and the player being played on shall be declared out. The ball is dead and all baserunners must return to the last base touched prior to the thrown ball hitting the bat or glove. (2) If the bat or glove belongs to the team in the field, it becomes a blocked ball and the overthrow rule applies. (3) If no apparent play is ob :ous, all runners will return to the last base touched at .ie time of the dead ball declaration. (Rule 1, Sec. 10).*

h. When a fair batted fly ball goes over the fence or into the stanc's, it shall entitle the batter to a home run, unless it passes out of the grounds at a distance less than the prescribed fence distances from home plate (as outlined in Rule 2, Section 1), in which case, the batter would be entitled to only two bases. The batter must touch the bases in regular order. The point at which the fence or stand is less than the distances listed (Rule 2, Section 1) from home plate shall be clearly marked for the umpire's information.

PLAY — *A fair batted ball touches (a) F9's glove and goes over the fence in fair territory, (b) F9's glove and goes over the fence in foul territory, (c) the top of a fence railing and goes over, (d) the top of a fence railing bounding to F9's glove and then over the fence in fair territory. RULING — A home run in (a) and (c), and a two-base hit in (b) and (d) based on Rule 8, Section 5i.*

i. When a fair ball bounds or rolls into a stand; over, under or through a fence; bounds out of play unintentionally off a defensive player or other obstruction marking the boundaries of the playing field.
EFFECT — Sec. 5i: The ball is dead and all baserunners are awarded two bases from the time of the pitch.
j. (1) When a live ball is unintentionally carried by a fielder from playable territory into dead ball territory, the ball becomes dead. All baserunners are awarded one base from the last base touched at the time "fielder" enters dead ball territory.

NOTE: A fielder carrying a live ball into the dugout or team area to tag a player is considered to have unintentionally carried it there.

(2) If, in the judgement of the umpire, a fielder intentionally carries a live ball from playable territory into dead ball territory, the ball becomes dead and all baserunners are awarded two bases from the last base touched at the time he entered dead ball territory.

NOTE: A dead ball line is considered in play.

Sec. 6. A BASERUNNER MUST RETURN TO HIS BASE:
a. When a foul ball is illegally caught and so declared by the umpire.
b. When an illegally batted ball is declared by the umpire.
c. When a batter or baserunner is called out for interference. Other baserunners shall return to the last base which was, in the judgement of the umpire, legally touched by him at the time of the interference.
d. (FP ONLY) When the plate umpire or his clothing interferes with the catcher's attempt to throw.

PLAY — With R1 attempting to steal, umpire interferes with catcher's throw. RULING — Umpire signals delayed dead ball. If R1 is not put out, umpire declares dead ball and R1 must return to the base he occupied before the interference.

e. When any part of the batter's person is touched by a pitched ball that is swung at and missed.
f. When a batter is hit by a pitched ball, unless forced.
g. When a foul ball is not caught.
EFFECT — Sec. 6a-g:
(1) The ball is dead.
(2) The baserunners must return to base without liability to be put out, except when forced to go to the next base because the batter became a baserunner.
(3) No runs shall score unless all bases are occupied.
(4) Baserunners need not touch the intervening bases in returning to base, but must return promptly; however, they must be allowed sufficient time to return.
h. (SP ONLY) Base stealing. Under no condition is a runner permitted to steal a base when a pitched ball is not batted. The runner must return to his base.
EFFECT — Sec. 6h: Baserunners may leave their bases when a pitched ball is batted or reaches home plate, but must return immediately after each pitch not hit by the batter. (16-inch SP ONLY) Baserunners may lead off prior to a pitched ball.
i. When a caught fair fly ball, including a line drive (FP and SP) or bunt (FP ONLY) which can be caught by an infielder with ordinary effort, is intentionally dropped with less than two outs and a runner on first base, first and second, first and third or first, second and third bases.

PLAY — REFER TO RULE 7, SECTION 11e EFFECT.

Sec. 7. BATTER-BASERUNNER IS OUT:
a. (FP ONLY) When the catcher drops the third strike and he is legally touched with the ball by a fielder before touching first base.
b. (FP ONLY) When the catcher drops the third strike and the ball is held on first base before the batter-baserunner reaches first base.
c. When, after a fair ball is hit, he is legally touched with the ball before he touches first base.
d. When, after a fair ball is hit, the ball is held by a fielder touching first base with any part of his person before the batter-baserunner touches first base.

PLAY — The first basemen has the ball in his right hand while lying on the ground. He touches first base with his left hand prior to the batter-baserunner reaching first base. RULING — The batter-baserunner is out.

e. When, after a fly ball is hit, the ball is caught by a fielder before it touches the ground or any object other than a fielder.
f. When, after a fair ball is hit, a base on balls is issued or the batter may legally advance to first base on a dropped third strike (FP ONLY), he fails to advance to first base and enters his team area.
EFFECT — Sec. 7a-f: The ball is in play and the batter-baserunner is out.
EXCEPTION: In slow pitch, the ball is dead and runners can not advance.

PLAY (1) — Batter hits ground ball to pitcher. Pitcher hesitates in throwing ball to first base. Batter, assuming he is an "easy out," enters his team area (bench, dugout, etc.). Pitcher finally throws to first base, but ball is not caught by first baseman and rolls into the dugout. Batter then leaves his team area and runs to first base. RULING — Batter is out.

PLAY (2) — REFER TO RULE 8, SECTION 1i.

g. When he runs outside the three-foot (0.91m) line and, in the judgement of the umpire, interferes with the fielder taking the throw at first base. However, he may run outside the three-foot (0.91m) line to avoid a fielder attempting to field a batted ball.
h. When he interferes with a fielder attempting to field a batted ball, intentionally interferes with a thrown ball or (FP ONLY) interferes with a dropped third strike. If this interference, in the judgement of the umpire, is an obvious attempt to prevent a double play, the baserunner closest to home plate shall also be called out.
i. When a batter-baserunner interferes with a play at home plate in an attempt to prevent an obvious out at home plate. The runner is also out.

PLAY — No outs. R1 on third base. Batter hits a ground ball to the first baseman then interferes with first baseman's throw to home plate for a play on R1. RULING — Batter and R1 are both declared out.

j. When he moves back toward home plate to avoid or delay a tag by a fielder.
k. When he is discovered using an altered or illegal bat.
EFFECT — Sec. 7g-k: The ball is dead and the batter-baserunner is out. Other baserunners must return to the last base legally touched at the time of or before the illegal action.

NOTE: In the case of an altered bat, the player is also ejected from the game.

Sec. 8. THE BASERUNNER IS OUT:
a. When, in running to any base, he runs more than three feet (0.91m) from a direct line between that base and the next one in regular or reverse order to avoid being touched by the ball in the hand of a fielder.
b. When, while the ball is in play, he is legally touched with the ball in the hand of the fielder while not in contact with a base.
c. When, on a force-out, a fielder tags him with the ball or holds the ball on the base to which the baserunner is forced to advance before the runner reaches the base.
d. When the baserunner fails to return to touch the base he previously occupied when play is resumed after suspension of play.
e. When a baserunner physically passes a preceding baserunner before that runner has been put out.
EFFECT — Sec. 8a-e: The ball is in play and the baserunner is out.

PLAY — With R1 on first, B2 hits a double. A throw to third drives R1 back to second. B2 has rounded second and discovers he has passed R1. He runs back and finally reaches first without being tagged out. RULING — B2 is out as soon as he passes R1.

f. When the baserunner leaves his base to advance to another base before a caught fly ball has touched a fielder, provided the ball is returned to a fielder and legally held on that base, or a fielder legally touches the baserunner before the baserunner returns to his base.

PLAY — No outs. R1 on third base. B2 hits fly ball to F7. F7 misjudges flight of ball and it hits him on the shoulder, deflects in the air to F8 and is legally caught by F8 before it hits the ground. R1 tags up at third base as soon as ball hits F7 on the shoulder but before F8 holds ball securely in glove. RULING — Legal advance. Run counts, R1 may leave base as soon as ball is touched.

g. When the baserunner fails to touch the intervening base or bases in regular or reverse order and the ball is in play and legally held on that base; or the baserunner is legally touched while off the base he missed.

PLAY (1) — With R1 on first, B2 hits safely to right field. An overthrow at first: (a) goes into the stand, (b) strikes the enclosing wall and rebounds to the catcher. In going to third base, R1 misses second base and has passed second or is approaching second when the ball leaves the hand of F9. The ball is then thrown to second for an appeal. RULING — In (a), if R1 has reached second base by the time the throw leaves the hand of F9, R1 is awarded home plate. If the appeal is properly made when the ball becomes alive, it should be allowed and the run scored by R1 is cancelled. If R1 has not reached second by the time the throw leaves the hand of F9, he is awarded third base. A proper appeal should be allowed and enforced. In (b), R1 is out on the appeal since the ball is not blocked, and no bases are awarded.

PLAY (2) — REFER TO RULE 1, SECTION 2.

h. When the batter-baserunner legally overruns first base, attempts to run to second base and is legally touched while off base.

PLAY — B1 reaches first safely but, in his overrun, he breaks for second then "gives up" while far away from the base line. RULING — If B1 is attempting to reach a base, he must be tagged, but the fielder is not expected to chase him into the outfield. In the outlined case, he is out for being out of the base line.

i. In running or sliding for home plate, he fails to touch home plate and makes no attempt to return to the base when a fielder holds the ball in his hand while touching home plate and appeals to the umpire for the decision.
EFFECT — Sec. 8f-i:
(1) These are appeal plays and the defensive team loses the privilege of putting the baserunner out if the appeal is not made before the next legal or illegal pitch.
(2) The ball is in play and the baserunner is out.

NOTE: On appeal plays, the appeal must be made before the next legal or illegal pitch, or before the defensive team has left the field. The defensive team has "left the field" when the pitcher and all infielders have clearly left their normal fielding positions and have left fair territory on their way to the bench or dugout area.

▶ (3) (16-INCH SP and FP ONLY) Baserunners may leave their base on live ball appeal plays when the ball leaves the eight foot (2.44m) radius around the pitcher's plate; or when the ball leaves the pitcher's possession; or when the pitcher makes a throwing motion indicating a play or fake throw. See Play 2 following Rule 8, Section 8u regarding fake throws.
▶ (4) (FP, SP, and 16-INCH) Once the ball has been returned to the infield and time has been called, any infielder (including the pitcher or catcher) with or without possession of the ball, may make a verbal appeal on a runner missing a base or leaving a base too soon. The administering umpire should acknowledge the appeal, and then make a decision on the play. Baserunners cannot leave their base during this period, as the ball remains dead until the next pitch.

NOTE: (a) If the pitcher has possession of the ball and is in contact with the pitching plate when making a verbal appeal, no illegal pitch is called. (b) If the umpire has indicated "play ball" and the pitcher now requests an appeal, the umpire would again call "time out" and allow the appeal process.

PLAY (1) — (FP, SP, and 16-INCH) Runner R2 leaves second base too soon on a fly ball caught by F7. The ball is thrown directly into the infield with an ap-

73

peal made by F4 at second base. RULING: The ball has remained alive and when properly appealed, R2 is called out.

PLAY (2) — *Runner R1 on second base and R2 on first base. Batter B3 hits a fly ball to F7. Both runners advance, however, R1 leaves too soon. Time is called. The pitcher has the ball and after the umpire recognizes the appeal, (a) the pitcher announces to the umpire he wants to appeal R1 leaving too soon, (b) the pitcher carries the ball over and touches R1 standing on third base, (c) the pitcher throws the ball to F4 who touches second base, or (d) the pitcher fakes a throw toward third base and the runner steps off the base. RULING: In all cases the ball is dead and baserunners cannot leave their base. (a) is the proper appeal; however (b) an (c) are acceptable.*

j. When the baserunner interferes with a fielder attempting to field a batted ball or intentionally interferes with a thrown ball. If this interference, in the judgement of the umpire, is an obvious attempt to prevent a double play and occurs before the baserunner is put out, the immediate succeeding runner shall also be called out.

PLAY — *With R1 on first, B1 hits the ball on the ground between first and second. R1 is struck by the batted ball or he hinders F4 in his throw to first. RULING — R1 is out and the ball becomes dead when the interference occurs. If the interference clearly prevented B2 from being put out at first, he also is out.*

k. When a baserunner is struck with a fair batted ball in fair territory while off base and before it passes an infielder, excluding the pitcher.

NOTE: Sec. 8j-k. When baserunners are called out for interference the batter-runner is awarded first base and credited with a base hit.

PLAY — *R1 is: (a) between second and third; or (b) touching second. He is struck by ball thrown by B3 before it passes a fielder. RULING — Ball becomes dead in (a) and (b). R1 is out in (a). He is not out in (b). The batter is entitled to first base in both cases.*

l. When a runner intentionally kicks a ball which an infielder has missed.
m. When, with a baserunner on third base, the batter interferes with a play being made at home plate with less than two outs.
n. *When anyone, other than another baserunner physically assists a baserunner while the ball is in play. On a batted fly ball the call should be made prior to the batted ball being caught or not caught, regardless of whether the ball is fair or foul, a delayed dead ball call will be made, the runner is out, and if the ball is caught, the batter is out. The ball becomes dead when the ball is caught or falls to the ground.*
o. When the coach near third base runs in the direction of home plate on or near the base line while a fielder is attempting to make a play on a batted or thrown ball and, thereby draws a throw to home plate. The baserunner nearest to third base shall be declared out.
p. When one or more members of the offensive team stand or collect at or around a base which a baserunner is advancing, thereby confusing the fielders and adding to the difficulty of making the play.

NOTE: Members of a team include bat boy or any other person authorized to sit on team's bench.

q. When the baserunner runs the bases in reverse order to confuse the defensive team, or to make a farce out of the game. (See Rule 8, Section 7j)
r. If a coach intentionally interferes with a thrown ball.
s. When the runner, after being declared out or after scoring, interferes with a defensive player's opportunity to make a play on another runner. The runner closest to home plate at the time of the interference shall also be declared out.
EFFECT — Sec. 8j-s: The ball is dead and the baserunner is out. Other baserunners must return to the last base legally touched at the time of or before the illegal action.

PLAY — *R1 on third base and R2 on first base. Batter hits a sharp grounder to second baseman who tags R2 out. In an attempt to throw to first base to retire the batter, R2 interferes with the second baseman. RULING — Ball becomes dead and R1 is also called out. Batter is awarded first base.*

t. When a defensive player has the ball and the runner remains on his feet and deliberately, with great force, crashes into the defensive player, the runner is to be declared out.
EFFECT — Sec. 8t: The runner is out, the ball is dead, and all other runners must return to the last base touched at the time of the collision, unless Rule 8, Section 8j or Rule 8, Section 8s applies.

NOTE: If the act is determined to be flagrant, the offender shall be ejected.

PLAY — *The catcher has received the ball and is waiting to tag the runner attempting to score. The runner deliberately runs into the catcher with great force, causing him to drop the ball. RULING — The runner is out. He is also ejected if the act is flagrant.*

u. (FP ONLY) When the baserunner fails to keep contact with the base to which he is entitled until the ball leaves the pitcher's hand. When a baserunner is legitimately off his base after a pitch or the result of a batter completing his turn at bat while the pitcher has the ball within an eight foot (2.44m) radius of the pitcher's plate, he must immediately attempt to advance to the next base or immediately return to his base.
(1) Failure to immediately proceed to the next base or return to his base once the pitcher has the ball within the eight foot (2.44m) radius of the pitcher's plate, will result in the baserunner being declared out.
(2) Once the runner returns to a base for any reason, he will be declared out if he leaves said base, unless a play is made on him or another runner (a fake throw is considered a play); the pitcher no longer has possession of the ball in the eight foot (2.44m) radius; or the pitcher releases the ball by a pitch to the batter.

NOTE: A base on balls or dropped third strike, on which the runner is entitled to run, is treated the same as a batted ball. The batter-baserunner may continue past first base and is entitled to run toward second base as long as he does not stop at first base. If he stops after he rounds first base, he then must comply with Section 8u(1).

PLAY — *With R1 on second, B2 takes a called third strike for the first out of the inning; meanwhile, R1 leads off second base after delivery to the plate. Catcher returns ball to the pitcher, who has the ball in the eight foot (2.44m) radius of the pitcher's plate. The runner at this moment makes no attempt to move either way. RULING — The runner must immediately return to second or immediately advance to the next base. Failure to immediately proceed to the next base or return to his base once the pitcher has the ball within the eight foot (2.44m) radius of the pitcher's plate, will result in the baserunner being declared out.*

v. (SP ONLY) When the baserunner fails to keep contact with the base to which he is entitled until a pitched ball has reached home plate or before the pitched ball is batted. EXCEPTION (16-INCH SP ONLY) Runners may leave their base as soon as the ball is declared in play.
EFFECT — Sec. 8u-v: The ball is dead, "NO PITCH" is declared and the baserunner is out.
w. When he abandons a base, does not attempt to advance to the next base, and enters the team area or leaves the field of play. The baserunner shall be declared out immediately when he enters the team area or leaves the field of play.
x. When the baserunner positions himself behind and not in contact with the base to get a running start on any fly ball, the runner is out and the ball remains live.

Sec. 9. BASERUNNER IS NOT OUT:

a. When a baserunner runs behind or in front of the fielder and outside the base line in order to avoid interfering with a fielder attempting to field the ball in the base path.
b. When a baserunner does not run in a direct line to the base, providing the fielder in the direct line does not have the ball in his possession.
c. When more than one fielder attempts to field a batted ball and the baserunner comes in contact with the one who, in the judgement of the umpire, was not entitled to field the ball.
d. When a baserunner is hit with a fair batted ball that has passed an infielder, excluding the pitcher, and in the judgement of the umpire no other infielder HAS A CHANCE TO MAKE AN OUT.

PLAY (1) — *With R1 on second, B2 hits ball behind F6 who is playing in. Batted ball touches R1 and is deflected into foul ground. RULING — If the touching of R1 is accidental, it is ignored because batted ball has passed a fielder. If R1 intentionally deflected batted ball, umpire will rule interference, with ball becoming dead and R1 being declared out.*

PLAY (2) — *A batted ball strikes third base then caroms into foul territory where it strikes R1, who is leading off third. RULING — R1 is not out and ball is in play since the ball was actually going away from the fielder.*

e. When a baserunner is touched with a ball not securely held by a fielder.
f. When the defensive team does not request the umpire's decision on an appeal play until after the next pitch.
g. When a batter-baserunner overruns first base after touching it and returns directly to the base.
h. When the baserunner is not given sufficient time to return to a base, he will not be called out for being off base before the pitcher releases the ball. No pitch will be called by the umpire (Rule 6, Section 9d.)
i. When a runner, who has legally started to advance, cannot be stopped by the pitcher receiving the ball while on the pitching plate nor by stepping on the plate with the ball in his possession.
j. When a baserunner holds his base until a fly ball touches a fielder, then attempts to advance.
k. When hit by a batted ball when touching his base, unless he intentionally interferes with the ball or a fielder making a play.

PLAY (1) — *With R1 on second, R2 on first and no outs, B3 hits a ground ball or infield fly. Ball strikes R1 who is: (a) near second, (b) standing on second. In both cases, ball has not passed an infielder. RULING — In (a), R1 is out on either type of hit. In (b), R1 is not out on either type of hit, but ball becomes dead and all runners, if forced, advance one base without liability to be put out. In both (a) and (b), B3 is out on any infield fly. If it is a ground ball, batter-baserunner is awarded first base.*

PLAY (2) — REFER TO RULE 8, SECTION 8k.

l. When a baserunner slides into a base and dislodges it from its proper position. The base is considered to have followed the runner.
EFFECT — Sec. 9l: A baserunner reaching a base safely will not be out for being off that base. He may return to that base without liability to be put out when the base has been replaced. A runner forfeits this exemption if he attempts to advance beyond the dislodged base before it is again in proper position.

PLAY — *R1 slides into second base. After he touches the base, he loses contact (a) because the base breaks lose from its fastening, (b) his foot slides off the base. F4 touches him while his foot is off base. RULING — In (a), R1 is not out. In (b), R1 is out.*

m. When a fielder makes a play on a batter or baserunner while using an illegal glove. The manager of the offended team has the option of having the entire play, including the batter's turn at bat, nullified with the batter batting over, assuming the ball and strike count he had before he hit the ball, and runners returned to the original bases they held prior to the batted ball, or taking the result of the play.
n. When the baserunner is hit by a fair batted ball after it is touched or touches any fielder, including the pitcher.

PLAY — *With R1 on second, B2 hits to F6 who is playing deep. Batted ball is touched by him and dropped so that it rebounds into R1. RULING — Touching of R1 is ignored since the ball has been touched by a fielder.*

74

RULE 9. DEAD BALL - BALL IN PLAY

Sec. 1. THE BALL IS DEAD AND NOT IN PLAY:
a. When the ball is batted illegally.

  PLAY — *R1 is on first base. B2 illegally bats the ball towards F6 and F4 obstructs R1, advancing to second base. RULING* — *Ball becomes dead when B2 illegally batted the ball. B2 is out and R1 must return to first base.*

b. When the batter steps from one box to another when the pitcher is ready to pitch.
c. When a ball is pitched illegally.
  EXCEPTION: Sec. 1c: (FP ONLY) If the pitcher completes the delivery of the ball to the batter, the batter hits the ball and reaches first base safely, and all baserunners advance at least one base, then the play stands and the pitch is no longer illegal. EXCEPTION: Sec. 1c (SP ONLY) If the batter swings at an illegal pitch, the play stands and the pitch is no longer illegal.
d. When "No Pitch" is declared.
e. When a pitched ball touches any part of the batter's person or clothing, whether the ball is struck at or not.

  PLAY — *B1 swings at a pitched ball and the ball hits his hand while holding the bat. RULING* — *Strike shall be called and the ball is dead. The hand is not considered part of the bat.*

f. When a foul ball is not caught.
g. When a baserunner is called out for leaving the base too soon on a pitched ball.
h. When the offensive team causes the interference.
  (1) When a batter intentionally strikes the ball a second time, strikes it with a thrown bat or deflects its course in any way while running to first base.
  (2) When a thrown ball is intentionally touched by a coach or on-deck batter.
  (3) When a fair ball strikes a baserunner or umpire before touching an infielder, including the pitcher, or before passing an infielder, other than the pitcher.
  (4) When the batter interferes with the catcher.
  (5) When a member of the offensive team intentionally interferes with a live ball.
  (6) When a runner intentionally kicks a ball which a fielder has missed.
  (7) (FP ONLY) When, with a baserunner on third base, the batter interferes with the play being made at home plate with less than two outs.
i. When the ball is outside the established playing limits of the playing area. A ball is considered "outside the playing field" when it touches the ground, person on the ground or object outside the playing area.

  PLAY — *R1 is on third. B3, at bat with one out, hits a fly ball which F5 catches in the field of play. F5's momentum causes him to go into a dead ball area, such as a bench, dugout, stands or beyond the chalk lines or pre-game determined imaginary line. RULING* — *Ball is dead as soon as F5 enters the dead ball area with the ball. R1 is awarded one base and B3 is out.*

j. If an accident to a runner prevents him from proceeding to a base which he is awarded. A substitute runner shall be permitted for the injured player.

  PLAY — *Batter hits ball over the fence for a home run and falls down as he attempts to advance to first base. Batter is injured and unable to continue to play. RULING* — *Substitue runner will be permitted for batter and will be allowed to circle the bases so that the home run can be allowed.*

k. In case of interference with batter or fielder.
l. (SP ONLY) When the batter bunts or chops the pitched ball.

  PLAY — *REFER TO RULE 7, SECTION 11l.*

m. (FP ONLY) When a wild pitch or passed ball goes under, over or through the backstop.
n. When time is called by the umpire.
o. When any part of the batter's person is hit with his own batted ball when he is in the batter's box.
p. When a baserunner runs bases in reverse order either to confuse the fielders or to make a travesty of the game.
q. When the batter is hit by a pitched ball.
r. When, in the judgement of the umpire, the coach near third base runs in the direction of home plate on or near the base line while the fielder is attempting to make a play on a batted or thrown ball, and thereby draws a throw to home plate.
s. (FP ONLY) When the plate umpire or his clothing interferes with the catcher's attempt to throw.
t. When one or more members of the offensive team stand or collect at or around a base which a baserunner is advancing, thereby confusing the fielders and adding to the difficulty of making a play.
u. (FP ONLY) When the baserunner fails to keep contact with the base to which he is entitled until a legally pitched ball has been released.
v. (SP ONLY) When a baserunner fails to keep contact with the base to which he is entitled until a legally pitched ball has reached home plate.
w. When a play is being made on an obstructed runner or if the batter-baserunner is obstructed before he touches first base.
x. (SP ONLY) After each strike or ball.
  EXCEPTION: The ball remains alive in 16-inch slow pitch.
y. When a blocked ball is declared.
z. When a batter enters the batter's box with or uses an altered bat.
aa. When a batter enters the batter's box with or uses an illegal bat.
ab. When a caught fair fly ball, including a line drive (FP and SP) or bunt (FP ONLY) which can be handled by an infielder with ordinary effort, is intentionally dropped with less than two outs and a runner on first base, first and second, first and third or first, second and third bases.

  PLAY — *REFER TO RULE 7, SECTION 11f.*

ac. When a fielder carries a live ball into dead ball territory.
  EFFECT — Sec. 1a-ad: The batter or baserunners may not advance on a dead ball unless awarded a base or bases by rule.
ad. When time has been called and an appeal is being made by the defense.

PLAY — *REFER TO RULE 8, SECTION 8i (4) AND PLAY 2.*

Sec. 2. THE BALL IS IN PLAY:
a. At the start of the game and each half inning when the pitcher has the ball while standing in his pitching position and the plate umpire has called "play ball."
b. (16-INCH SP ONLY) When the ball becomes dead and it is apparent to the umpire that an appeal play is going to be made. The ball will be put in play when the pitcher is within eight feet (2.44m) of the pitcher's plate with the ball in his possession and the plate umpire calls "play ball." The batter does not have to take his place in the batter's box on an apparent appeal play, however, the defensive players must take a position on fair ground, with the exception of the catcher who must be in his box.
c. When the infield fly rule is enforced.

  PLAY — *With one out, R1 is on second and R2 on first when B4 hits an infield fly. Baserunners are of the opinion two were out and they start running as soon as the ball is hit. F4 fails to catch the infield fly and both runners cross home plate. RULING* — *B4 is out for hitting infield fly, but runs count since runners may advance at their own risk.*

d. When a thrown ball goes past a fielder and remains in playable territory.
e. When a fair ball strikes an umpire or baserunner on fair ground after passing or touching an infielder.
f. When a fair ball strikes an umpire on foul ground.
g. When the baserunners have reached the bases to which they are entitled if the fielder fields a batted or thrown ball with illegal equipment.
h. When a baserunner is called out for passing a preceding runner.
i. When no play is being made on an obstructed runner. The ball shall remain alive until the play is over.
j. When a fair ball is legally batted.
k. When a baserunner must return in reverse order while the ball is in play.
l. When a baserunner acquires the right to a base by touching it before being put out.
m. When a base is dislodged while baserunners are progressing around the bases.
n. When a baserunner runs more than three feet (0.91m) from a direct line between that base and the next one in regular or reverse order to avoid being touched by the ball in the hand of a fielder.
o. When a baserunner is tagged or forced out.
p. When the umpire calls the baserunner out for failure to return and touch the base when play is resumed after a suspension of play.
▶ q. When a live ball appeal play is legally being made.
r. When the batter hits the ball.
s. When a live ball strikes a photographer, groundskeeper, policeman, etc., assigned to the game.

  PLAY — *B1 hits a line shot which hits first base, ricochets off the bag and hits photographer who is assigned to take pictures of the game. Pitcher backs up play and throws out B1 advancing to second. RULING* — *B1 is out. Ball remains in play when it strikes a photographer who has been assigned to the game.*

t. When a fly ball has been legally caught.
u. When a thrown ball strikes an offensive player.
v. If the batter drops the bat and the ball rolls against the bat in fair territory and, in the judgement of the umpire, there was no intention to interfere with the course of the ball. The batter is not out and the ball is alive and in play.
w. When a thrown ball strikes an umpire.
x. Whenever the ball is not dead, as provided in Section 1 of this rule.
y. When a thrown ball strikes a coach.
z. (FP and 16-INCH SP ONLY) When a ball has been called on the batter. When four balls have been called, the batter may not be put out before he reaches first base.
aa. (FP and 16-INCH SP ONLY) When a strike has been called on the batter.
ab. (FP and 16-INCH SP ONLY) When a foul tip has been legally caught.

  PLAY — *Does the ball become dead after a foul tip, and can there be a foul tip which is not caught? RULING* — *The ball does not become dead for a foul tip and a runner may advance or be put out the same as after any strike. To be a foul tip, the ball must be caught by the catcher.*

ac. (SP ONLY) As long as there is a play as a result of the hit by the batter. This includes a subsequent appeal play.
ad. (FP and 16-INCH SP ONLY) If the ball slips from a pitcher's hand during his wind-up or the backswing.

Sec. 3. (SP ONLY) THE BALL REMAINS ALIVE UNTIL THE UMPIRE CALLS "TIME," WHICH SHOULD BE DONE WHEN THE BALL IS HELD BY A PLAYER IN THE INFIELD AREA AND, IN THE JUDGEMENT OF THE UMPIRE, ALL PLAY HAS CEASED.

RULE 10. UMPIRES

NOTE: Failure of umpires to adhere to Rule 10 shall not be grounds for protest. These are guidelines for umpires.

Sec. 1. POWER AND DUTIES. The umpires are the representatives of the league or organization by which they have been assigned to a particular game; and, as such, are authorized and required to enforce each section of these rules. They have the power to order a player, coach, captain or manager to do or to omit any act which, in their judgement, is necessary to give force and effect to one or all of these rules; and to inflict penalties as herein prescribed. The plate umpire shall have the authority to make decisions on any situation not specifically covered in the rules. THE FOLLOWING IS THE GENERAL INFORMATION FOR UMPIRES:
a. The umpire will not be a member of either team (i.e. player, coach, manager, officer, scorer or sponsor).
b. The umpire should be sure of the date, time and place of the game and should arrive at the playing field 20-30 minutes ahead of time, start the game on time and leave the field when the game is over. His jurisdiction begins when he enters the field to

check the bats, and ends when he leaves the field following the third out of the last inning.

c. A male umpire shall wear a powder blue shirt, long or short sleeved, dark, navy blue trousers and cap. A female umpire shall wear a powder blue blouse, long or short sleeved, and dark, navy blue, full length slacks. A cap is not required for a female umpire. All other paraphernalia (i.e. socks, ball bag, jacket and/or sweater) must also be dark, navy blue, and the shoes and belt must be black for both male and female umpires. A t-shirt is optional to wear under the powder blue shirt, however, if one is worn, it must be white. The plate umpire, whether male or female, in fast pitch MUST wear a black mask with a black throat protector. It is recommended that he wear a mask behind the plate in slow pitch also. Body protectors are recommended for umpires in fast pitch and are optional in slow pitch.

d. The umpires should introduce themselves to the captains, managers and scorers.

e. The umpire should inspect the playing field boundaries, equipment and clarify all ground rules to both teams and their coaches.

f. Each umpire will have the power to make decisions on violations committed anytime during playing time or during suspension of play until the game is over.

g. No umpire has the authority to set aside or question decisions made by another umpire within the limits of his respective duties, as outlined in these rules.

h. An umpire may consult his associate at any time. However, the final decision will rest with the umpire whose exclusive authority it is to make the decision and who requests the opinion of the other umpire.

i. In order to define "respective duties," the umpire judging balls and strikes will be designated as the PLATE UMPIRE, the umpire judging base decisions will be designated as the BASE UMPIRE.

j. The plate umpire and base umpire will have equal authority to:
(1) Call a runner out for leaving a base too soon.
(2) Call "TIME" for suspension of play.
(3) Remove a player, coach or manager from the game for violation of rules.
(4) Call all illegal pitches.

k. The umpire will declare the batter or baserunner out, without waiting for an appeal for such decision, in all cases where such player is retired in accordance with these rules.

NOTE: Unless appealed to, the umpire will not call a player out for having failed to touch a base, leaving a base too soon on a fly ball, batting out of order or making an attempt to go to second after reaching first base, as provided in these rules.

l. The umpire will not penalize a team for infraction of a rule when imposing the penalty would be to the advantage of the offending team.

Sec. 2. THE PLATE UMPIRE SHOULD:

a. Take a position behind the catcher. He will have full charge of and be responsible for the proper conduct of the game.

b. Call all balls and strikes.

c. By agreement and in cooperation with the base umpire, call plays, fair or foul balls, legally or illegally caught balls. On plays which would necessitate the base umpire leaving the infield, the plate umpire will assume the duties normally required of the base umpire.

d. Determine and declare whether:
(1) A batter bunts or chops a ball.
(2) A batted ball touches the person or clothing of the batter.
(3) A fly ball is an infield or an outfield fly.

e. Render base decisions as indicated in the Umpire's Manual.

f. Determine when a game is forfeited.

g. Assume all duties when assigned as a single umpire to a game.

Sec. 3. THE BASE UMPIRE SHOULD:

a. Take such positions on the playing field as outlined in the Umpire's Manual.

b. Assist the plate umpire in every way to enforce the rules of the game.

Sec. 4. RESPONSIBILITIES OF A SINGLE UMPIRE. If only one umpire is assigned, his duties and jurisdiction will extend to all points. He will take a position in any part of the field, which, in his judgement, will best enable him to discharge his duties.

Sec. 5. CHANGE OF UMPIRES. Umpires cannot be changed during a game by the consent of the opposing teams, unless an umpire is incapacitated by injury or illness.

Sec. 6. UMPIRE'S JUDGEMENT. There will be no appeal from any decision of any umpire on the grounds that he was not correct in his conclusion as to whether a batted ball was fair or foul, a baserunner safe or out, a pitched ball a strike or ball, or on any play involving accuracy of judgement; and no decision rendered by any umpire will be reversed, except when he is convinced it is in violation of one of these rules. In case the manager, captain or either team does seek reversal of a decision based solely on a point of rules, the umpire, whose decision is in question, will, if in doubt, confer with his associates before taking any action. But under no circumstances will any player or person, other than the manager or captain of either team, have any legal right to protest any decision and seek its reversal on a claim that it is in conflict with these rules.

a. Under no circumstances will any umpire seek to reverse a decision made by his associates; nor will any umpire criticize or interfere with the duties of his associates, unless asked to do so.

b. The umpire-in-chief may rectify any situation in which the reversal of an umpire's decision or a delayed call by the umpire places a batter-runner or a baserunner in jeopardy.

PLAY — *With R1 on first base and less than two outs, the runner steals with the pitch (FP ONLY). The catcher throws to second base as the plate umpire calls ball four. The throw is in time and the base umpire calls the runner out. As the runner (R1) leaves for the dugout, the base umpire realizes B2 has four balls and R1 is entitled to second base. The defense tags R1 when he leaves the base. Had the umpire not called R1 out, he would not have left the base. RULING — Place R1 on second base and B2 on first base.*

Sec. 7. SIGNALS:

a. **SAFE** — Body upright, eyes on the ball and arms extended straight out with the palms down. A verbal call of "Safe" is made as the arms are snapped to this position from the upper chest.

b. **SAFE SELL** — The same as the safe call, but as the arms are extended straight out with the palms down, a step should be taken towards the play.

c. **OUT** — Body upright, eyes on the ball and right arm extended straight up as an extension of the shoulder. As we come to the 'HAMMER' position, the elboy is bent at a 90° angle and the fist closed with the fingers facing the right ear. The left arm should be brought to the mid-section of the body. A verbal call of "Out" is made as the right arm is extended high in the air and continued as the arm drops into the 'HAMMER' position.

d. **OUT SELL** — Come to up-right position and take a step with left foot directly at the play. Your head should remain in position looking at the play as the upper torso turns perpendicular from the play. Raise right arm with an open hand behind your head into a throwing position as you shuffle your right foot behind the left. Plant right foot and transfer weight, bringing right arm over the top of your head with a closed fist, making a vigorous 'OUT' call. Finish call by transferring your weight to the left foot while bringing the right foot forward and parallel to the left.

e. **STRIKE** — Body upright, eyes on the ball and right arm extended straight up as an extension of the shoulder. As we come to the 'HAMMER' position, the elbow is bent at a 90° angle and the fist is closed with the fingers facing the right ear. The left arm should be brought to the mid-section of the body. A verbal call of "Strike" is made as the right arm is extended high in the air and continued as the arm drops into the 'HAMMER' position.

f. **FAIR BALL** — Body upright, eyes on the ball, make a pumping motion toward fair territory with the arm that is toward the infield. There is no verbal call on a fair ball and if the umpire is wearing a mask it should be in the left hand.

g. **FOUL BALL** — On all foul balls, except a caught foul fly ball, the ball is DEAD and the DEAD BALL signal should be given preceeding the foul ball signals. For the FOUL BALL signal, body should be upright, eyes on the ball extending the arm straight out from the shoulder toward foul territory away from the playing field. A verbal call of "FOUL BALL" should be made as the arm motion is made.

h. **TIME OUT/DEAD BALL** — Body upright, the arms are both extended high in the air with the palms of the hand open and facing away from the umpire's body. A verbal call of "Time" or "Dead Ball" is made at the same time the arms are going up.

i. **PLAY BALL** — Body upright, eyes on the ball, the umpire makes a motion toward the pitcher with the right hand. A verbal call of "Play" or "Play Ball" is made as the umpire motions toward the pitcher.

j. **HOLD UP PLAY** (No Pitch) — Body upright, raise either hand with the palm facing the pitcher. On a right handed batter use the right hand, and on a left handed batter, use the left hand. "NO PITCH" shall be declared if the pitcher pitches while the umpire has a hand in said position.

k. **DELAYED DEAD BALL** — Body upright, the left arm is extended straight out to the side of the body as an extension of the shoulder and the left hand is in a fist. This position is held long enough for the players to see that the umpire has observed the act that pre-empted this call.

l. **INFIELD FLY** — Body upright, eyes on the ball, extend the right arm high in the air with a closed fist. Make a verbal of "Infield Fly". If the batted ball is near the foul line call "Infield Fly, If Fair".

m. **TRAPPED BALL** — Same as safe signal except the umpire makes a verbal call of "No Catch" instead of saying "Safe".

n. **FOUL TIP** — Body upright, eyes on the ball, the fingers of both hands are touched together then the umpire gives the strike signal with no verbal call. This indicates that the bat tipped the ball and was caught by the catcher.

o. **COUNT** — Body upright, have eye contact with the pitcher, both hands are extended high above the head and use the fingers to indicate the ball and strike count on the batter. Use the fingers on the left hand for "Balls" and the fingers on the right hand for "Strikes". A verbal description of the count on the batter is given while the hands are overhead and "Balls" are always mentioned first and "Strikes" second.

p. **DOUBLE** — body upright, raise the right hand high above the head, indicating with two fingers, the number of bases awarded. A verbal call of "Two Bases" is made while the hand remains overhead.

q. **HOME RUNS** — Body upright, raise the right hand high above the head with a closed fist and make a counter-clockwise circling motion with the raised hand. A verbal call of "Four Bases" is made at the same time the hand is overhead.

Sec. 8. SUSPENSION OF PLAY:

a. An umpire may suspend play when, in his judgement, conditions justify such action.

b. Play will be suspended whenever the plate umpire leaves his position to brush the plate or to perform other duties not directly connected with the calling of plays.

c. The umpire will suspend play whenever a batter or pitcher steps out of position for a legitimate reason.

d. An umpire will not call "time" after pitcher has started his windup.

e. An umpire will not call "time" while any play is in progress.

f. In case of injury, "time" will not be called until all plays in progress have been completed or runners have been held at their bases.

g. Umpires will not suspend play at the request of players, coaches or managers until all action in progress by either team has been completed.

PLAY — *Bases are full. B4 hits a long fly to center. F7 and F8 collide in trying to make the catch and both are injured. All runners cross home plate. Captain requests "time" to prevent the last two runs from scoring. RULING — Ball does not become dead when a player is injured during a batted or thrown ball. Umpire will not call "time" until no further play is possible. All four runs count.*

h. (SP ONLY) When, in the judgement of an umpire, all immediate play is apparently completed, he should call "time."

Sec. 9. VIOLATIONS AND PENALTIES:

a. Players, coaches, managers or other team members will not make disparaging or insulting remarks to or about opposing players, officials or spectators; or commit other acts that could be considered unsportsmanlike conduct.

b. There will be no more than two coaches for each team to give words of assistance and direction to the members of their team while at bat. One coach should be stationed near first base and the other near third base. They must remain in their coach's box.

c. The penalty for violations by a player is prompt removal of the offender from the game and grounds. For the first offense, coach or manager may be warned; but for the second offense, he is removed from the game. The offender should go directly to the dressing room for the remainder of the game or leave the grounds. Failure to do so will warrant a forfeiture of the game.

RULE 11. PROTESTS

Sec. 1. PROTESTS WILL NOT BE RECEIVED OR CONSIDERED IF THEY ARE BASED SOLELY ON A DECISION INVOLVING THE ACCURACY OF JUDGEMENT ON THE PART OF AN UMPIRE. Examples of protest which will not be considered are:
a. Whether a batted ball was fair or foul.
b. Whether a baserunner was safe or out.
c. Whether a pitched ball was a strike or a ball.
d. Whether a pitch was legal or illegal.
e. Whether a baserunner did or did not touch a base.
f. Whether a baserunner left his base too soon on a caught fly ball.
g. Whether a fly ball was or was not caught legally.
h. Whether it was or was not an infield fly.
i. Whether there was or was not interference or obstruction.
j. Whether the field is fit to continue or resume play.
k. Whether there is sufficient light to continue play.
l. Any other matter involving only the accuracy of the umpire's judgement.

Sec. 2. PROTESTS THAT SHALL BE RECEIVED AND CONSIDERED CONCERN MATTERS OF THE FOLLOWING TYPES:
a. Misinterpretation of a playing rule.
b. Failure of an umpire to apply the correct rule to a given situation.
c. Failure to impose the correct penalty for a given violation.

Sec. 3. PROTESTS MAY INVOLVE BOTH A MATTER OF JUDGEMENT AND THE INTERPETATION OF A RULE.
EXAMPLE:
With one out and runners on second and third, the batter flies out. The runner on third tags up after the catch and the runner on second does not. The runner on third crosses the plate before the ball is played at second base for the third out. The umpire does not allow the run to score. The questions as to whether the runners left their bases before the catch and whether the play at second base were made before the runner on third crossed the plate, are solely matters of judgement and are not protestable. It is a misinterpretation of a playing rule when the umpire failed to allow the run to score and is a proper subject for protest.

Sec. 4. THE NOTIFICATION OF INTENT TO PROTEST MUST BE MADE IMMEDIATELY BEFORE THE NEXT PITCH. (EXCEPTION: Player eligibility)

PLAY (1) — R1 is obstructed in a rundown between first and second bases by F4 while being played on. Umpire rules OBSTRUCTION and returns R1 to first base. Offensive team protests game (a) before first pitch to B2, (b) after first pitch to B2, (c) after game is over. RULING — (a) Protest is valid. In (b) and (c), protest is denied since it was not made before the next pitch.

PLAY (2) — Bases loaded, bottom of seventh inning, two outs, and the score is visitors 4, home 3. Home team (offensive) coach calls a second conference with a batter in that half inning. The plate umpire calls the batter out and the game is called. Both teams are off the playing field and preparing to leave when the home manager protests to the umpire in the parking lot that the ruling was incorrect. RULING — The game is over. When both teams have left the playing field, no protest can be accepted.

a. The manager or acting manager of the protesting team shall immediately notify the plate umpire that the game is being conducted under protest. The plate umpire shall in turn notify the opposing manager and official scorekeeper.
b. All interested parties shall take notice of the conditions surrounding the making of the decision which will aid in the correct determination of the issue.

NOTE: On appeal plays, the appeal must be made before the next pitch, legal or illegal, or before the defensive team has left the field. For the purpose of this rule, the defensive team has "left the field" when the pitcher and all infielders have left fair territory on the way to the bench or dugout area.

c. *Once the game is completed and both teams have left the field, no protest can be filed. EXCEPTION: Player eligibility.*

Sec. 5. THE OFFICIAL WRITTEN PROTEST MUST BE FILED WITHIN A REASONABLE TIME:
a. In the absence of a league or tournament rule fixing the time limit for filing a protest, a protest should be considered if filed within a reasonable time, depending upon the nature of the case and the difficulty for obtaining the information on which to base the protest.
b. Within 48 hours after the scheduled time of the contest is generally considered a reasonable time.

Sec. 6. THE FORMAL WRITTEN PROTEST SHOULD CONTAIN THE FOLLOWING INFORMATION:
a. The date, time and place of the game.
b. The names of the umpires and scorers.
c. The rule and section of the Official Rules or local rules under which the protest is made.
d. The decision and conditions surrounding the making of the decision.
e. All essential facts involved in the matter protested.

Sec. 7. THE DECISION MADE ON A PROTESTED GAME MUST RESULT IN ONE OF THE FOLLOWING:
a. The protest is found invalid and the game score stands as played.
b. When a protest is allowed for misinterpretation of a playing rule, the game is replayed from the point at which the incorrect decision was made, with the decision corrected.
c. When a protest for ineligibility is allowed, the team shall forfeit the game being played or the game last played to the offended team.

RULE 12. SCORING

NOTE: Failure of official scorer to adhere to Rule 12 shall not be grounds for protest. These are guidelines for the official scorer.

Sec. 1. THE OFFICIAL SCORER SHALL KEEP RECORDS OF EACH GAME AS OUTLINED IN THE FOLLOWING RULES. He shall have sole authority to make all decisions involving judgement. For example, it is the scorer's responsibility to determine whether a batter's advance to first base is the result of a hit or an error. However, a scorer shall not make a decision which conflicts with the Official Playing Rules or with an umpire's decision.

Sec. 2. THE BOX SCORE:
a. Each player's name and the position or positions he has played shall be listed in the order in which he batted or would have batted, unless he is removed or the game ends before his turn at bat.
▶ (1) (FP ONLY) The designated player (DP) is optional, but if one is used, it must be made known prior to the start of the game, and be listed on the scoresheet in the regular batting order. Ten names will be listed, with the tenth name being the player playing defense only. This tenth player can only bat if he moves to the 'DP' position in the batting order, and this would then terminate the role of the 'DP'.
EXCEPTION: See Rule 4, Section 3c.
(2) (SP ONLY) The extra player (EP) is optional, but if one is used, it must be made known prior to the start of the game, and be listed on the scoring sheet in the regular batting order. Eleven names for men's and women's slow pitch and twelve names for Co-Ed slow pitch will be on the official batting order.
NOTE: If a DP or EP is used, he must be used the entire game. Failure to complete the game with a DP or EP results in forfeiture of the game. EXCEPTION: See Rule 4, Section 3c.
b. Each player's batting and fielding record must be tabulated.
(1) The first column will show the number of times at bat by each player, but a time at bat will not be charged against the player when:
(a) He hits a sacrifice fly that scores a runner.
(b) He is awarded a base on balls.
(c) (FP ONLY) He hits a sacrifice bunt.
(d) (FP ONLY) He is hit by a pitched ball.
(e) (FP ONLY) He hits a sacrifice slap bunt. NOTE: A slap bunt is defined as a fake bunt, followed by a controlled swing, resulting in the runner advancing as would be the case with a sacrifice bunt.
(2) The second column will show the number of runs made by each player.
(3) The third column will show the number of base hits made by each player. A base hit is a batted ball that permits the batter to reach base safely:
(a) On a fair ball which settles on the ground, clears the fence or strikes the fence before being touched by a fielder.
(b) On a fair ball which is hit with such force or such slowness, or takes an unnatural bounce, making it impossible to field with ordinary effort in time to retire the runner.
(c) When a fair ball, which has not been touched by a fielder, becomes "dead" because of touching the person or clothing of an umpire.
(d) When the fielder unsuccessfully attempts to retire a preceding runner, and in the scorer's judgement, the batter-baserunner would not have been retired at first base by perfect fielding.
(4) The fourth column will show the number of opponents put out by each player.
(a) A putout is credited to a fielder each time he:
(1) Catches a fly ball or line drive.
(2) Catches a thrown ball which retires a batter or baserunner.
(3) Touches a baserunner with ball when the baserunner is off the base to which he is entitled.
(4) Is nearest the ball when a runner is declared out for being struck by a fair ball or interference with the fielder, or when a runner is called out for being in violation of Rule 8, Section 8u and Section 8e.
(b) A putout is credited to the catcher:
(1) When a third strike is called.
(2) (SP ONLY) When the batter bunts or chops the ball downward.
(3) When the batter fails to bat in correct order.
(4) When the batter interferes with the catcher.
(5) The fifth column shall show the number of assists made by each player. An assist shall be credited:
(a) To each player who handles the ball in any series of plays which results in the putout of the baserunner. Only one assist shall be given to any player who handles the ball in any putout. A player who has aided in a rundown or other play of the kind shall be credited with both an assist and a putout.
(b) To each player who handles or throws the ball in such a manner that a putout would have resulted except for an error of a teammate.
(c) To each player who, by deflecting a batted ball, aids in a putout.
(d) To each player who handles the ball in a play which results in a baserunner being called out for interference or for running out of base line.
(6) The sixth column will show the number of errors made by each player. Errors are recorded:
(a) For each player who commits a misplay which prolongs the turn at bat of the batter or life of the present runner.
(b) For the fielder who fails to touch the base after receiving the ball to retire the runner on a force-out or when a baserunner is compelled to return to base.
(c) For the catcher, if a batter is awarded first base for interference.
(d) For the fielder who fails to complete a double play because of dropping the ball.
(e) For the fielder, if a baserunner advances a base because of his failure to stop or try to stop a ball accurately thrown to a base, providing there was occasion for the throw. When more than one player could receive the throw, the scorer must determine which player gets the error.

Sec. 3. A BASE HIT SHALL NOT BE SCORED:
a. When a runner is forced out by a batted ball or would have been forced out except for a fielding error.
b. When a player fielding a batted ball retires a preceding runner with ordinary effort.

77

c. When a fielder fails in an attempt to retire a preceding runner and, in the scorer's judgement, the batter-baserunner could have been retired at first base.

Sec. 4. A RUN BATTED IN IS A RUN SCORED BECAUSE OF:
a. A safe hit.
b. A sacrificed bunt (FP) or sacrifice fly (FP and SP).
c. A caught foul fly.
d. An infield putout or fielder's choice.
e. A baserunner forced home because of interference or the batter being hit with a pitched ball or given a base on balls.
f. A home run and all runs scored as a result.

Sec. 5. A PITCHER SHALL BE CREDITED WITH A WIN:
a. When he is the starting pitcher and has pitched at least four innings and his team is not only in the lead when he is replaced, but remains in the lead for the remainder of the game.
b. When a game is ended after five innings of play and the starting pitcher has pitched at least three innings, and his team scores more runs than the other team when the game is terminated.

Sec. 6. A PITCHER SHALL BE CHARGED WITH A LOSS, REGARDLESS OF THE NUMBER OF INNINGS HE HAS PITCHED, IF HE IS REPLACED WHEN HIS TEAM IS BEHIND IN THE SCORE AND HIS TEAM, THEREAFTER, FAILS TO TIE THE SCORE OR GAIN THE LEAD.

Sec. 7. THE SUMMARY SHALL LIST THE FOLLOWING ITEMS IN THIS ORDER:
a. The score by innings and the final score.
b. The runs batted in and by whom.
c. Two base hits and by whom.
d. Three base hits and by whom.
e. Home runs and by whom.
f. Sacrifice flies and by whom.
g. Double plays and players participating in them.
h. Triple plays and players participating in them.
i. Number of bases on balls given by each pitcher.
j. Number of batters struck out by each pitcher.
k. Number of hits and runs allowed by each pitcher.
l. The name of the winning pitcher.
m. The name of the losing pitcher.
n. The time of the game.
o. The names of the umpires and scorers.
p. (FP ONLY) Stolen bases and by whom.
q. (FP ONLY) Sacrifice bunts.
r. (FP ONLY) The names of batters hit by a pitched ball and the name of the pitcher who hit them.
s. (FP ONLY) The number of wild pitches made by each pitcher.
t. (FP ONLY) The number of passed balls made by each catcher.

Sec. 8. (FP ONLY) STOLEN BASES ARE CREDITED TO A BASERUNNER WHENEVER HE ADVANCES ONE BASE UNAIDED BY A HIT, PUTOUT, FORCE-OUT, FIELDER'S CHOICE, PASSED BALL, WILD PITCH, AN ERROR OR ILLEGAL PITCH.

Sec. 9. ALL RECORDS OF A FORFEITED GAME WILL BE INCLUDED IN THE OFFICIAL RECORDS EXCEPT THAT OF A PITCHER'S WON-LOST RECORD.